SCENES FROM
A SOMERSET CHILDHOOD
Llewelyn Powys

REDCLIFFE
Bristol

First published in 1986 by
Redcliffe Press Ltd, 49 Park Street, Bristol 1

ISBN 0 948265 55 8

*Typeset and printed in Great Britain by
Penwell Ltd, Parkwood, Callington, Cornwall*

CONTENTS

Publisher's note

This evocation of country life in the late nineteenth century is a compilation of essays by Llewelyn Powys which first appeared, in book form, as follows:

A Baker's Dozen—The Village Shop, A Montacute Field, The Memory of One Day, Tintinhull, Childhood Memories, Montacute Hill and A Somerset Christmas. *Somerset Essays*—Memory Stirred (as Albert Reginald Powys), Montacute House, Nancy Cooper, Exmoor, Ham Hill, and Pitt Pond. *Dorset Essays*—Weymouth in the Three Eights.

Acknowledgements

The publisher wishes to thank all those who have kindly supplied advice and photographs. Credits for photographs are as indicated, except for those not captioned: pages 30 and 33, Ann Clarke; page 45, Joan Astell.

Paul Roberts' introduction is published by courtesy of *Somerset and Avon Life*.

INTRODUCTION

T he family into which Llewelyn Powys was born on August 13th, 1884, was surely one of our most outstanding literary families; one which can be compared in importance only to that of the Brontes, and which produced, in addition to Llewelyn, both John Cowper and Theodore Francis Powys, two of our most unique and remarkable novelists.

Though he was born at Rothesay House in Dorchester, Llewelyn was less than 18 months old when his father became vicar of Montacute and the family moved to the Somerset village which was to be the centre of his life for the next 29 years.

These were to be years of great happiness and Llewelyn would frequently spend his days exploring the surrounding countryside with one or another of his ten brothers and sisters. It was just such an outing as this that he was to recall in his essay *A Somerset Christmas*:

"My brother Bertie and I would begin to be aware of the approach of Christmas even before the end of the autumn term at Sherborne. We used, I remember, to walk to a certain holly tree growing in the field to the right of Babylon Hill from which we could look across the town of Yeovil to the leafless outlines of Odcombe, Montacute Hill, Hedgecock, and Ham Hill fretted in a miniature landscape of the wintry western horizon . . .

"No Christmas Day could have been passed more simply and innocently than ours was at Montacute Vicarage, and yet in retrospect every moment of it seems to have been full of an incredible golden happiness . . . All the day long my brother and I would have been busy collecting, in two large baker's baskets, moss and fir branches for the church and holly and mistletoe for our own home."

Throughout all the years that he was later to spend travelling abroad it was to Montacute that his memory turned and, as he wrote towards the end of his life:

"Often I may appear to be studiously contemplating the sun-lit snowfields of the Alps, when all the while through the swift agency of the inward eye, I am in reality revisiting in my imagination familiar country spots in the neighbourhood of the village of Montacute."

In 1895 Llewelyn was sent, following the family tradition, to Sherborne Preparatory School where his brother Littleton was later to establish himself so successfully as headmaster. Though he was academically rather slow, his sunny disposition and sporting prowess made him popular with the other boys and these again were happy years.

Again following the footsteps of his ancestors Llewelyn went to Cambridge where, in 1903, he took over the rooms previously occupied by his brother John Cowper, who had now become a strong and lasting influence on him. However, the question of what Llewelyn was to do with his future was now becoming more urgent. Certainly, though he tried hard to develop his faith in Christianity, he could not follow his father into the church, and it was more or less by accident that he drifted into teaching. Yet fears of his own inadequacy and his temperamental unsuitability for the work depressed him deeply and he drifted from post to post becoming increasingly disheartened and apathetic.

John Cowper Powys had by now established a fine reputation as a lecturer in America and the opportunity to join him lifted Llewelyn's spirit. He worked furiously to prepare for his lectures but again the venture proved unsuccessful and Llewelyn returned to Montacute more deeply depressed than ever.

It was then, on November 3rd, 1909, that the most decisive event of Llewelyn's life occurred. Echoing the words of Keats he wrote in his diary:

"There is blood in my mouth. That drop of blood is my death warrant."

Later he was to describe this period of his life, and his subsequent attempts to find a cure in Switzerland, in his book *Skin for Skin*, in which he wrote:

"All through that autumn I had been troubled by a bad cold, by a cold of that particularly virulent kind, persisting week after week, which is common enough in an English countryside where for months on end people inhale mists, move about in chilled rooms, and sleep between damp sheets. I had been lying awake for hours, and never for a single moment had the rain ceased from lashing against the windowpanes of my bedroom, never for a moment had the wind ceased beating against the walls of the house, that wind which I knew, but a few minutes before, had been passing over Lenty Common, over Silver Lake, and over the lonely stretches of the Bradford Abbas road.

"Suddenly, after a fit of coughing more violent than usual, an ugly conviction came over me that something was wrong. I lit a candle and discovered that my mouth was full of blood. The next day my worst misgivings were confirmed by a doctor. I was found to be suffering from pulmonary tuberculosis."

He had suffered from a weak chest since childhood but the discovery that he had tuberculosis, though it was to cast a shadow over the rest of his life, was also to spur on this aimless young man of 25 to begin his life's work. In his own words it 'sharpened his wits' and now he began in earnest to write the essays and books which were later to bring him fame.

Following the death of his mother in 1914, Llewelyn travelled to Kenya to take over from his brother Willie as manager of a huge sheep farm, hoping that the climate would help to cure him. He was to stay there for almost five years and his experiences are vividly recounted in *Black Laughter*, a collection of essays and stories which, when they were originally published in *The New York Evening Post*, first brought him the recognition that he had come to deserve.

From 1920 until 1925 Llewelyn lived in America and described his life there in another remarkable book *The Verdict of Bridlegoose*. It was here also that he met the writer Alyse Gregory who was then managing editor of *The Dial*, one of the most influential literary magazines of its day. They were married in New York on September 30th, 1924, and in May of the following year they returned to England and established their home at The White Nose on the Dorset coast.

Powys was to spend much of the remaining 14 years of his life travelling and writing and he produced many fascinating books in which he combined his acute observation of nature and his deep, almost magical sense of history and tradition with an urgent and unsentimental enjoyment of life. The epicurean and life-embracing philosophy which he developed in defiance of his illness is best expressed in *The Glory of Life*, first published in 1938, though for many it is in collections of essays such as *Thirteen Worthies, Earth Memories* and *Dorset Essays*, that his genius is most surely displayed.

But the fascination of Powys lies not only in the subject of his writing but in the elegance and beauty of his style, which has a quality which marks him out as not only a writer of individual genius but as part of a long tradition of English writers. He was, as John Cowper Powys put it, 'a born stylist', and any reader coming new to his work will soon find himself drawn into the world he recreates, a world in which he celebrates both his philosophy and his life, for one cannot exist without the other. In writing of 'Ham Hill', 'Wookey Hole' or such intriguing characters as the eccentric 17th-century traveller Tom Coryat from Odcombe, or the 18th-century composer and poet Thomas Shoel of Montacute, Powys invariably finds something of universal importance while at the same time staying firmly rooted in local soil.

Llewelyn Powys died at Davos Platz in Switzerland on the morning of December 2nd, 1939, and yet, in the books he left behind him, he remains an urgent and exciting voice and one who, regardless of fashion, will not be forgotten.

PAUL ROBERTS

The Powys family at the Vicarage, Montacute, around 1910. Llewelyn is in the front row, on the right. The vicarage was Llewelyn's home for twenty nine years, and in later life his mind constantly returned to the security and happiness he enjoyed there. 'In those laughing hours,' he wrote, 'it was impossible to think of life as ever ending.' (Photo: E.E. Bissell)

MEMORY STIRRED

Thou'lt come no more, never, never, never,
never, never!

A FEW SUMMERS AGO I WAS PRESENT AT THE REDEDICATION CERE-
mony of the little church of Winterbourne Tomson, which, with
money realised from the sale of one of Thomas Hardy's
manuscripts, had been restored under the personal care of my brother, Mr
A R Powys. I well remember observing my brother moving about amongst
the officiating clergy and assembled people, a man easily distinguished by
the sincerity and vigour of his presence. He was evidently well pleased by
the accomplishment of the task he had taken in hand. Today he lies buried
on the south side of this same church.

We had been warned that he was very ill and I dreaded lest I should hear
the tread of the man who brings us our telegrams. When the message came
the actual shock affected me in a way that I had not anticipated. All that
had happened to us during the last thirty years seemed to fall into a fading
distance, while with the abruptness of a lantern slide every incident of my
boyhood we had spent together stood out bold and clear.

At the back of the kitchen garden wall of Montacute Vicarage was a plot
of pear trees and under their shadows we used to play. My brother
Theodore had been the first to take possession of this section of the
garden, and with characteristic originality had occupied himself with
digging deep holes and underground passages in the firm clay a few feet
below the surface soil. These subterranean labyrinths I can only just
remember. When he and my brother John began to shoot with forbidden
pistols, using the apple trees in the lower orchard as targets, the pear tree
plot came presently to be regarded as belonging to my brother Bertie, my
sister May, and myself. There had always existed a rough lean-to shed
against the high wall, and this we little by little rebuilt and extended,
giving it the name of the May-Ber-Lulu Castle.

During my life whenever I have wished to regain serenity it has been my
habit to direct my thoughts to this playground of my childhood. Even
when I have been in bed with a high fever I have been able to quiet my
pulse by reviving my memories of this parcel of enchanted ground.

We were very fond of forget-me-nots, and our miniature borders were
crowded with this lovely childish flower. It was an ordinary forget-me-not,
except that each tiny individual head was larger than is usual and of a very
light hue. As I came racing round the corner of the kitchen garden, past
the July apple tree, and saw these pools of blue, the sodden Somerset soil
might have been subjected to some airy transmutation associated with the
sky above the outspreading garlands of the milk-white blossoms of the
fruit trees.

My brother Littleton, long before I could remember, had devised a hole
in the wall to serve as a nesting place for tits, and these bright little birds,

with the faces of diminutive owls and a plumage almost tropical, would be for ever flitting through the patched sunny shadows on some dancing quest of happy spring-time discipline.

At Sherborne, my brother Bertie used to save all his money for buying posts and matchwood-boarding and tiles and bricks for our Maberlulu 'improvements'. My own nature was never as stable as his and I was never very good at saving. While he would spend hours in the school workshop carpentering I would be eating chocolates at Ford's as shamelessly insatiable as a yellow guinea-pig over a saucer of bran. He was never one to care about dress and I can see him now standing by a chess table that he was making, his waistcoat covered with sawdust, his trousers baggy at the knee, gravely concentrating with brown, long-fingered, sensitive hands upon his work, and yet glad to see me also, even though he was well aware I had only appeared with ingratiating manners to beg pennies from him. This chess table was a masterpiece of carpentering skill, the squares formed alternately out of ebony and boxwood, but, alas! when it reached Montacute with our other luggage and was unpacked by us *it was broken*. I was a very small boy, but I remember as I saw the tears suddenly begin to flow from the eyes of my brother, always so proud and reserved, my very marrow bones melted with a longing to be able to comfort him. We sat, I recollect, side by side on the drawing-room sofa, with the singing of the birds coming in to us through the wide open sash window so loud that the familiar room might have belonged to a summer bower in a Sultan's aviary at Nishapour rather than to a Victorian vicarage in England. A few days before he died I experienced the same desire to protect him when he ended a letter with the words 'My whole love. A.R.P.'

How tender he always was of me at school. At Wilson's House he shared a study with a rather conventional boy in whose presence we never dared to be demonstrative. Many a time I have loitered in the boot-room at the end of the narrow passage outside the studies waiting for this worldly-minded athlete, with his grand velvet caps, to come out, so that I might slip silently into the little room knowing that my brother Bertie would take me upon his knee and we would talk of home, sitting on a dusty cushion-padded cane chair in front of his fire. With what competent conscientious thoroughness he used to plan out every detail for our return to Montacute at the end of each term! To gain a few hours he would ask leave for us to get up early on the long anticipated morning, and we would walk to Yeovil with our black school handbags, packed with our home-made night-gown and brush and comb, swinging in our hands.

On one of these occasions a worldly London boy took it into his head to see us off. He walked with us across the field behind the Preparatory, my brother keeping up as best he could the 'hard talk' of the school world, and I following behind silent.

He left us at the field gate where the girls' school now stands quite unmindful that his departure, straw hat nonchalantly tilted on the back of his head, marked the real beginning of our holidays, with freedom to kiss

Montacute Vicarage today, now known as Park House.   (Photo: Ann Clarke)

without being laughed at, and with freedom to talk about our sisters without fear of being overheard.

As we trudged up Half-way-hill and along by Col. Goodden's palings, released at last to plan eagerly together about the new Maberlulu roof, how happy, how happy we were, with the small birds singing in the hedges, and the lords-and-ladies unfolding in the ditches, and with the scárcely credible prospect dancing before us in our minds of being home so very soon, with our mother leaving her sewing to welcome us, her face illumined, at the front door, and our father coming out of the study into the dining-room to listen to our excited talk; with Rogers mowing the lawn for the first time, and one or two hyacinths already out in the round beds. I remember that the new roof of the Maberlulu had become so important to us that when the wood we had selected with such economic foresight from the timber yard of Mr Drayton came we were up long before dawn to begin the work, my brother driving in his three-inch nails with the precision of a capable carpenter, but I, less expert, adding the anguish of hammered fingers to the unexpected discomfort of sunless unwarmed winds.

We kept an alarm clock in the 'end room' where we slept, and often before the bell rang for family prayers we would have already enjoyed many hours of an April day. If there was no particular work to be done on the Maberlulu we would go for long bird-nesting walks, following one behind the other beating the green hedges, bright and shining with dew as the level sun rays touched each leaf of the shrouded West Country trees. How fresh created the coverts and woods would seem as we stole into them long before the keeper Parsons had left his lonely house surrounded by kennels of fierce fast-chained black retriever dogs; and how they smelt of cool-shadowed mossy swards, and rang with the songs of the newly awakened birds. With our boots soaked and muddy we would sit very hungry waiting for the servants to come in for family prayers, and our father, doubtless remembering early morning expeditions of his own through the Stalbridge meadows, would say, as he rubbed his hands together with a look of extra-ordinary good nature: 'Well, my boys, I see you have been out early'. On one of these walks we actually went searching for the sources of the River Parrett in fields that my father did not even know, in fields far away beyond the Chinnocks. These long, long walks by the side of my brother left on my mind a peculiar glamour so that the sensation of extreme physical exhaustion when walking in the open country has never since been disliked by me.

It was my custom in the summer holidays to spend all my birthday money at Miss Sparkes's shop. I would buy pots and pans and crockery for the Maberlulu, selecting with the utmost care the mugs and plates I liked best, and then run all the way back, so eager would I be to present my purchase to my brother and sister whom I would perhaps find enjoying the refreshment of some of our home-made ginger beer which we used to drink out of teacups sitting on the seat of our new bow window. Or perhaps as I came round the corner I would see my sister in her red overall stirring a mess of Quaker oats for my birthday feast on a wood fire in the little yard, Bertie kneeling at her side selecting the exact, right-shaped sticks to put under the pot. The smoke would be mingled with the smell of the flowers lying upon the air in that sheltered spot, as the heat of the midday sun increased. In after years whenever I have smelt burning wood, whether from the bonfires of broken boxes that the little boys of New York love to build on the kerbs of Greenwich village streets, or from camp fires in Africa where the tree hyraxes call, or from black Bedouin goathair tents near the Lake of Galilee, in a single instant my spirits would be freed from ordinary time and space restrictions to be transported, swift as any Ariel, back to the Maberlulu.

By the first week of September the wall-fruit would begin to ripen. In earlier days it had been my mother's custom at this season to appear in the nursery with an apricot or peach and to gather us about her like little birds with wide open mouths to receive in strictest turn portions of the sun-sweetened food dipped in dessert-sugar and transfixed, all dripping, on the end of a silver ivory-handled fork. As we grew older we learned to pick the fruit from the trees ourselves. I can remember doing this on Sunday evenings with Japanese anemones in the button-holes of our dark suits, and with the church bells just beginning to chime, their silver sound hardly noticed by us as we searched for hidden greengages, with hollows of sweetness edged brown by the maws of wasps, wasps which at the first sign of being disturbed would, with yellow striped abdomens curled towards their heads, drop from leaf to leaf, hopelessly inebriate and yet still apt to mischief.

These were the weeks when we all would play at 'Jabberwock', a game invented by my brother John, with the acacia on the top lawn as 'home'. With what fleet feet, tennis-shoe shod, we would race along the terrace-walk and up the narrow garden path by Willie's wood, and across the lawns slippery with dew; while every moment the garden grew dimmer and dimmer, an incense-breathing garden populated by creatures fabulously fitted with goblin eyes for seeing in the dark, owls that flew silently out of the leafy obscurities of the sycamore, bats that flickered with high-toned cries to and fro above the drive, and nectar-sipping moths with back and wings fur-covered, sumptuous and soft as silk, exploring with fixed stare each lavender spike and each yellow cavern of the evening primroses now no longer limp. In those laughing hours it was impossible to think of life as ever ending, so reassuring was the sound of tittering lovers at the back gate, and the trit-trot of horses' feet growing fainter along the dusty Stoke road; and with the light of the lamp, its shade painted by my sister Gertrude, shining steadily from the drawing-room window, where our mother sat reading to our father as he worked quietly at his netting, a string firmly looped over one black slipper.

In the Christmas holidays all was different. We scarcely visited the Maberlulu then. Always we were eagerly waiting for it to freeze or snow, looking up continually at the cowl on the top of the 'end-room' chimney so as not to miss the very first indication that it was swinging round to the north-east, a cowl that was more dented than the helmet of Achilles by our lucky idle hits with leaden slugs from the catapults that my brother was so good at making out of forked sticks chosen from the tall privet hedge surrounding the out-of-door earth closet. When the frost did come at last we would race round the garden in the early morning along the banked up celery mounds as hard as iron and stand first on the ice on the tank, and then on the ice on the butt, so that at breakfast we could report how hard the frost had been.

Then after Bible reading we would rush off to the Montacute Hill ponds in the hope that they might already bear. When the night came we would be running out of the back-door every few minutes to look at the thermometer hung up by the study window and to put more and more water on the slide, which we always made in the yard above the tool-house, so that it would be ready for the next morning. How cold it would be in our room at the end of the passage on such nights! My brother had been given a large flat red candlestick which was kept on our dressing table, and the last in bed had to blow it out and get himself safe under the clothes before the glowing spark of the wick was no longer to be seen. What pleasure there was too in getting our skates out from the schoolroom cupboard in order to sandpaper them and see that their leather straps were in order! They were the old-fashioned skates with great rusty screws protruding, which when Pitt Pond was reached the next morning would be affixed by the help of a gimlet into the heels of our boots.

Gone, gone, gone, my brother who shared with me my childhood memories and forgot nothing! Who is able now to tell me whether the apple tree in which we found our hawfinch's nest is still standing? Who can now explain to me why it was the kites we used to make with long paper tails never flew properly, hold them against the wind and run as fast as we might? Who now could go to the beech tree that overlooks the Trent valley from where the best view of the Montacute and Odcombe range of hills is to be got, and from the white part of which we used to dislodge the little excrescences called by us 'eyes', taking them away as tokens of the lessening number of school weeks?

When he was lying sick in what proved to be his death-bed I sent him my essay on the Montacute poet and musical composer, Thomas Shoel. In the essay I explain that the village of Montacute is sheltered on the west by Ham Hill. 'This,' he wrote, after his abrupt manner, 'is not true. *In fact it is a lie.*' This roughness in the interest of truth was as characteristic of him as it was when, at the end of his letter, he described Shoel with singular imaginative sympathy as being 'like a rare autumn crocus crushed in the print of an ox's hoof.' It was the last communication that was ever to pass between us, and it was in this letter that he ended with the words 'My whole love. A.R.P.'

I remember as though it were yesterday when he first decided to be an architect. We were sitting sketching in Stoke Churchyard surrounded by grey tombstones. And now he who always had so deep a regard for the past lies himself buried, all his exceptional knowledge of wood and stone stored up during his life, utterly lost, of no more avail in man's economies than the dust of a buried stock.

The first work in his profession he supervised was the repairing and enlarging of a little schoolhouse at Longload. He had then been in Mr Benson's office but a few weeks, and I remember the expression of supreme satisfaction on his boy's face as he watched the Ham Hill stones being lifted into their proper positions. It would be difficult to calculate the number of walls belonging to every period of human building that have since received the informed and dedicated attention of 'this giant of quiet good works.' That afternoon marked the beginning of a career of great value to the country. It was perhaps his obstinate sincerity, a sincerity never to be budged, that gave so much weight to his judgements as secretary for the Society for the Protection of Ancient Buildings. All the views he held were integrated by a single individual attitude of mind, a vigorous philosophic attitude of mind that was continually directed upon the whole stream of his sense-impressions.

Bishopston, Montacute, c.1900. Miss Sparkes's village shop was on the right. (Photo: Alan Clark) Below, the shop as depicted by Llewelyn's sister, Gertrude.

THE VILLAGE SHOP

THE OTHER DAY I UNEXPECTEDLY RECEIVED AS A PRESENT A LARGE antiquated photograph of my old home in the county of Somerset. There to the life the familiar vicarage stood with its slate roof and French shutters and jasmine, rose-muffled walls, a four-square shadowed reality that seemed most worthily to represent the easy period to which it belonged. It was not, however, so much the large-sized picture itself that arrested my attention as the two words—Deborah Sparkes—written in a bold hand on the cardboard back of the faded photograph. Though Miss Sparkes has now been dead for many years I remember the old lady well. Indeed, of all the village characters of my childhood she perhaps holds a more prominent position than any. And even if the woman's personality had not been as dominating as it was, she must still have played an important part in the life of my father's parish, for in those days the owner of the village shop of very necessity was a person of consequence.

Although she had lived in Somerset for so many years Miss Sparkes was not, to use the proud exclusive cottage phrase, 'one of Montacute'; she originally had come from Devonshire where she had belonged, so it was rumoured, to a substantial Quaker family. Let this be as it may, while Miss Sparkes was a woman who held strong and independent views on every subject under the sun, yet she was strictly conventional, and never once can I recollect having seen her pew empty in my father's church. Her scrupulous honesty was also a byword in the village. In her accounts the unexplained presence of so much as a farthing could become a matter of the gravest concern. Miss Sparkes's shop was most fortunately situated in the very middle of Bishopston, one of the main streets of Montacute. You mounted two steps of Ham Hill stone worn uneven by I know not how much house-wifely shoe leather, turned an easy rattling door handle, and immediately found yourself plumb in the centre of what in fact was a mart of universal provision for the creature wants of the rural stone-quarrying population of the locality.

The shop contained two counters, the one on the left being devoted to the dispensing of sweets and groceries, and the one on the right to the selling of dry goods—flannels, calicos, laces, tapes, and 'what maids lack from head to heel'. Both of these plain, well-worn, spotlessly clean counters were provided with pocket-knife-made slots, the one slot cut with precision for the reception of coppers, and the other for white money. To be allowed to drop payment coins through these homely apertures, and to listen for their jingling fall into the drawer below, became for me a most coveted privilege. The sweets sold were of three varieties—bullseyes, acid drops, and almonds out of a glass bottle, covered with pink and white sugar. The biscuit most in favour was called Osborne. It was a round and wholesome cracker, though one that was a trifle dangerous on the occasion of a coughing fit because of its dry crumbs.

Miss Sparkes had a maid called Emma. I never observed, however, that she was allowed to play a very active part in the salesmanship of the shop. She was a humble little woman, born, so it seemed, to receive with a silent and saintly patience hasty rebukes for petty errors, petty inaccuracies, and for leaving undone what she ought to have done. Besides Emma this small establishment maintained one other inmate—Miss Sparkes's nephew, a mysterious middle-aged man of reserved deportment who was kept very much in the background. He was never, for example, permitted to meddle with village affairs and was seldom, if ever, to be seen in the street. His duties were severely confined to the large garden that lay behind the little house, a garden that stretched up as far as the wall that separated the potato plots at the backs of the houses from Mile's Hill field.

What a garden it was over which the refined, reticent man presided! In the summer time, if the shop happened to be empty of customers, Miss Sparkes would sometimes, as a treat, lead me into this unlikely paradise. There was a small lawn above her green water-butt yard, and at the end of this stood a modest arbor of the kind that John Bunyan might have meditated in—and wonder beyond all wonder, suspended near it, from a pear tree branch, was a large cage containing a talking parrot:

> *My name is parrot, a bird of Paradise*
> *With my becke bent, my little wanton eye,*
> *My fethers fresh, as is the emraude grene,*
> *About my neck a circulet, lyke the ryche rubye,*
> *My little legges, my fete both nete and cleane.*
> *Parrot is no stamring stare, that men call a starling,*
> *But Parrot is mine own dere hart, and my darling.*

Never, never could I hope to express how exciting it used to be to me suddenly to hear the bird's Caribbean screams when it first caught sight of its mistress, slow foot after slow foot, mounting the garden steps. It was a talking parrot—and how its reiterations of 'Pretty Poll,' 'Pretty Poll' would sound shrilly out amongst the wealth of globed peonies, larkspurs, and hollyhocks all in a row. Miss Sparkes, still holding me by the hand, would open the cage door and coax the parrot to sit upon her finger, a fabulous popinjay some of whose feathers were of as pure gold as those I read about in the fairy tales, a gilded emerald bird utterly besotted with love for the old, old woman whose features, indeed, looked not dissimilar to its own, so hooked and headstrong was the nose upon which her spectacles of shining steel were balanced.

> *Indie hath of kinde such as will counterfaite redily a*
> *mans speach: what wordes they heare, those commonly*
> *they pronounce. There have bene found of these that have*
> *saluted Emperours.*

Abbey Farm, and St Catherine's Church, Montacute.　　　(Photo: Ann Clarke)

Over the red-tiled roof of the shop it was possible to see the tall perpendicular tower of St Catherine's, and what a striking contrast it made, this homely English garden so suggestive of long dozing Sunday afternoons, with this outlandish darling of the fo'c's'le—penants and plumes of tropical flame! The parrot was almost pilled and must have been a bird of very great age. Perhaps it had been brought to England by one of Nelson's sailors from Antigua, for I have often fancied that Miss Sparkes in her maidenhood had had a romantic attachment with some able-bodied seaman who had perhaps visited the river mouths of half the known world:

> *O hold your tongue, my pretty parrot!*
> *Nor tell no tales o' me!*
> *Your cage shall be made o' the beaten gold*
> *And the spokes o' ivorie.*

One of her most valued possessions was, I know, a seaman's ditty box, out of which, upon occasions, when her mood was gay, she would select for me the most unexpected presents. One of these I still have, a carved ornament from China representing a hideous oriental priest astride a frog, who, with demonic grin, thonged whip in hand, is mercilessly lashing the reptile's bulging abdomen.

> *Pol is a fine bird! O fine lady Pol!*
> *Almond for parrot. Parrot's a brave bird.*

The parrot died before Miss Sparkes herself. It was buried in the quiet garden, the chosen plot of ground being marked the next summer by a carefully prepared flower-knot of London pride, marjoram, melilot, and that most lovely of old-fashioned pinks, sops-in-wine.

In these days the small shopkeepers are being hard put to it to make a living, and yet how excellently, and with what a sense of social responsibility, they have performed their modest offices in the past. It was the custom of Miss Sparkes each summer to undertake a journey to Bristol for the purpose of replenishing her shop with goods for a twelvemonth. She would return by the evening train, which, at a leisurely speed, would meander back to Yeovil by Athelney withybeds and through the sunset hayfields of Langport coming at last to a standstill at the Montacute station. Miss Sparkes, having first superintended the husbanding of her packages in the waiting room, would never fail to hasten along the platform past the quartz-bordered flower beds already cooled by the first dew fall, to where, in calm dignity, the locomotive rested. With ceremonious courtesy she would awaken the good natured engine driver from his idle dreamings by gravely bestowing upon him her personal thanks for having brought her, Deborah Sparkes, out of Sedgemoor, safely back once more to the peaceful village of her life-long adoption.

Cutting withies, at Athelney.   (Photo: Somerset Rural Life Museum)

A MONTACUTE FIELD

... O wild-raving winds! if you ever do roar
By the house and the elms from where I've a-come,
Breathe up at the window, or call at the door,
And tell you've a-found me a-thinking of home.

WILLIAM BARNES

THE MINDS OF BANISHED MEN WILL OFTEN REVERT TO THEIR DIS-
tant homes. A dozen times in a day they will be haunting in rever-
ies the fields, lanes, hills, and woodland banks of their childhood
memories. I know it is constantly so with me. Often I may appear to be
studiously contemplating the sun-lit snow fields of the Alps, when all the
while through the swift agency of the inward eye, I am in reality revisiting
in my imagination familiar country spots in the neighbourhood of the
village of Montacute.

Most of all in these mental wanderings does my mind remember every
sloping contour of a certain historical field situated beyond Batemoor, on
the foot-path-way towards Bagnel, the most outlying farm of the parish.
The name of the large romantic field is Witcombe, and that good physician
and gifted antiquarian, the late Dr Hensleigh Walter, used to tell me that a
mediaeval hamlet once flourished upon its acres. At the time of the Black
Death all its inhabitants died and the steading was never again re-
established. To this day it is possible, when the light falls in a certain
fashion, either in the late afternoon or during the first hour after dawn, to
detect where some of the old dwellings stood, cottages probably little
better than rough sheds of wattle and daub, with roofs thatched with
grass, straw, or reed from the marshlands that bordered the nearby stream
of drinking water.

Somerset was one of the counties that suffered severely from the
terrifying pestilence, possibly on account of the entertainment by the
Bristol merchants of some of those wandering brigs of disaster, which,
loaded down to their gunwales with cargos of richest treasure, had been
compelled to keep to the high seas, beaten away from every port of Europe
with horror and dread and merciless ferocity. Bristol was in the fourteenth
century the second city of England, and, with the exception perhaps of
Norwich, it became more plague-stricken than any other town of the realm.
The shocking mortality which accompanied this dire sickness from the
Orient, with its horrible symptoms of shivering, blood-spitting, and
blackening glands, followed by sudden death, fell heaviest on the poor, the
well-to-do being not only free to fly before the face of the scourge, but also
physically in better case to resist its ravages when attacked. The Bishop of
Bath and Wells, for example, prudently avoided the more populous
districts of his diocese, quickly retiring to one of the smallest of his
manors, his manor at Wiveliscombe. The plague, it is now believed, was

communicated by the rat-carried black flea. It rapidly spread over the whole of England: 'There was no more care for dying folk than men would care nowadays for goats.' Scarcely would the Montacute death-bell cease from tolling for one departing soul than it would boom out again for another: 'All men that hear my mournfull sound repent befor you lye in ground'. The poem by Thomas Nashe *In the Time of Pestilence*, though composed at a later visitation, gives us an excellent idea of the prevailing mood on the occasions of such awful epidemics:

> *Adieu, farewell earth's bliss!*
> *This world uncertain is;*
> *Fond are life's lustful joys*
> *Death proves them all but toys.*
> *None from his darts can fly;*
> *I am sick, I must die—*
> *Lord, have mercy on us!*

The cattle wandered free upon Chinnock Ridge, the corn was left unharvested and the young man who made merry with an unexpected legacy on Monday, lay mute in the churchyard's yellow clay by the time the sacring-bell of St Catherine's was heard to tinkle on the following Sunday; and everywhere 'for fear and horror, men scarcely dared to practise the works of piety and mercy—that is, to visit the sick and bury the dead . . . throughout our scattered villages and homesteads the wretched labourers and poor folks, with their families: . . . died by the roadside, or among their crops or in the cottages . . . not only did the speaking or association with sick folk bring disease to the sound, or involve both in one common death, but even the touch of their clothes, or anything else which the sick had touched and handled, seemed in itself to convey the same sickness to him who had touched.'

Witcombe, the field of these dolorous memories, is situated behind Batemoor Barn a little southward of the old coaching road of the West Country, which, passing the ancient hostelry at Pye Corner, runs through Odcombe and so over Ham Hill to Exeter. The valley on its eastern side is sheltered by Horses' Covert, and on the west by Norton Covert. It is a veritable vale of springtime. In April Witcombe echoes every few minutes to the mocking laughter of the woodpecker, as in lifting flights it casts a glancing volatile shade across the green turf, close-cropped by mild eyed sheep from the Abbey Farm. On both sides of the field's steep slopes the gorse grows in dark masses rendering the air balmy-soft in this windless sanctuary of sheltered peace. No field near Montacute is better placed for hearing the cuckoo for the first time, or indeed for seeing the first swallow, fresh in from the restless wastes of sea beyond Golden Cap. How the air of Witcombe can tremble with the songs of linnets—the breast feathers of the small birds daintily flushed—one madrigal answering another from prickly spray to prickly spray! Witcombe is also remarkable for its wild daffodils, short stalked native flowers that have made glad the hearts of I know not how many Montacute children; rejoicing also elderly village women from Bishopston and Middlestreet, good, understanding women, with a sound homespun culture that comes from reading deep rather than wide, who have walked up here by the Batemoor footpath for their first spring holiday. I have always believed these daffodils to be the descendants of those that once grew in the gardens of the ruined hamlet, and I suspect the same lineage belongs to the plants of hellebore to be found here, a flower much prized by mediaeval herbalists as a cure against headaches and all melancholy vapours.

How peerless these pastoral slopes can seem at Easter time! It was in the old withy-bed below the field called on maps by the beautiful name of Bride's Mead, that our nurse Emily would gather the pussy willows she loved so much, leaving the family perambulator—a broad beamed open conveyance constructed to carry three children sitting up side by side—in the safe harbourage of some hedge-shelter; and allowing us our freedom in the jungle of moss and marsh-marigolds, thrushes' nests and newly arrived chiff-chaffs.

Gone, gone, gone, all gone, the near past, together with the far past; yet there must be even now many morsels of obdurate matter—trinkets, arrow-heads, shards—beneath the sod that would tell of the breathing country people who laughed and wept and called and sang under these fair green hills six hundred years ago. How many generations of Montacute people must have returned to the sweet sequestered village up through these peaceful acres from Tinker's Bubble! The eighteenth century Montacute poet, Thomas Shoel, must have come this way time and again, and before him footsore monks returning to the Abbey from pedestrian visits with scrip and staff into Devonshire, and always and always the humble field-labourers of each patient age.

Surely truth is to be found in the old words of wisdom 'Oure life shall passe awaye as the trace of a cloude, and come to naught as the myst that is dryven awaye with the beames of the Sonne, and put downe with the heate thereof. Oure name also shall be forgotten litle and litle, and no man shall have oure workes in remembrance.' As insubstantial as drifting mist we pass, one and all, across earth's lucky grass, never to bide in one stay; and there was, perhaps, no little reason in that man who made himself merry at the expense of Death, calling him to naught for being but 'a foolish devourer of fretful shadows.'

Country life around the turn of the century. *Opposite*: women working in the Somerset fields. *Following pages*: ploughing with oxen and horses, and threshing with a flail (Photos: Somerset Rural Life Museum/Museum of the English Rural Life, University of Reading)

THE MEMORY OF ONE DAY

I N THE YEAR 1899 I AND MY YOUNGER BROTHER WERE TAKEN ILL WITH whooping cough. This tedious sickness was possibly in my case responsible for a lifelong weakness of the chest, but at the time nothing but good fortune seemed to come of the malady. We were sent home from Sherborne, and to our great delight our father decided that the seaside air of Weymouth might do us good.

Lodgings were found in Brunswick Terrace and even now when I enter one of these happy holiday houses, so sedate and so unostentatious, there are revived within me fleeting shadowy sensations of that far off Easter-time, with the small hallway of our house smelling of sand, of sun-dried seaweed, of cooking fish; and our sitting-room upstairs so safe and cheerful, where, in warm lamplight, we would listen to our sister Gertrude reading to us 'Wee Sir Gibby' as we sipped our bedtime milk different from Somerset milk—richer and more chalky white—with always the sound of the waves breaking on shingle coming in to us through the sash-window, opened a little at the top.

Our coughs did not at all interfere with our freedom. I recall, for example, looking for birds' nests on Lodmoor before breakfast and carrying my brother on my back over many of its wide shallow lagoons, indifferent to wet boots and stockings. It has pleased me to remember this service, for how often when we were in Africa together did I not take advantage of his strength and of his love for me, accepting it as natural that I could leave it to him to off-saddle my pony when, tired and stiff, at the end of a long trek, I would limp away, speechless, to some shady resting place.

Almost every day during this visit we would plan out some excursion—to Portland Bill, to Upwey Wishing Well, to the Swannery at Abbotsbury—returning in time for our tea which we used to take at a table drawn close up to the bow-window eating our eggs, honey, watercress, and brown bread looking out over the water at the undulating line of familiar cliffs stretching away as far as St Alban's Head. White Nose especially awakened our imaginings. Many times we tried to guess what it was actually like on that grave promontory whose smooth green westward slopes were to be seen, even in detail, by the naked eye. Each evening it confronted us, patient and strong in the daffodil light, with its suggestion of sailor boys home from the sea, of the frigates of Nelson's time tipping over the horizon, and of huge wooden merchantmen coming back to England from the West Indies, weeds from the Sargasso Sea still clinging to their carved rudders.

We made a plan to walk to White Nose, or to the White Nore, as it used to be called by the Victorian gentlefolk. The day we selected for this most adventurous of all our expeditions was fine. It was one of those supreme days of an English April that brings to everything that lives an uncontrollable sense of well-being. The sky was clear and every coach-road shimmered at its far end with sun motes; the downs smelt of gorse, the meadows of daisies; and the whole earth fainted and danced, now enervated, now awakened by the breathless allure of a spring morning.

We ate our provisions at the look-out at the top of the White Nose sitting under the shadow of a little stone house, the roof of which was a heavy upturned fishing boat that had long ago been captured from the smugglers and now was as soundly leaded against the weather, keel and sides, as the top of any church tower. All was strange, as strange as though we had found ourselves lodged upon some ledge of remote altitude on one of those cumulus clouds which on indolent summer afternoons would remain stationary for hours above the garden lawn teasing our childhood fancies. The view from the great cliff was different from anything we knew about. The sea was blue, the sky was blue. The waves were white, the cliffs were white—white, blue—blue, white; and the air we breathed of a salty crystal quality, softened with fragrance of downland flowers. Far up above the sprouting cornland behind us the larks trilled with tireless ecstasy.

I was sent, I remember, to the old coastguard station to beg a jug of water. The present coastguard station had not yet been built. In its place was a row of firm one-storied wooden houses shining with pitch and white paint, each garden path bordered with white-washed stones similar in weight and shape to those that in Victorian times used to encircle the coast of England for the better safety of the vigilant excise men on their midnight assignations. Some of these stones, matted over with grass, are still to be observed on the cliff's edge.

In those quiet days, Ringstead remained uninvaded and unspoilt, and I recall well how we wandered across its flat acres, amazed to find ourselves in cowslip fields, the greeness of which showed bright as in a painted picture, bright against an azure sea, whose salt waves in rough weather, must, so we judged, splash upon the grass and buttercups of the meadows. From the beech trees of the woods where the old pirate-destroyed thirteenth century village once had been, a cuckoo was calling; and in the secret gardens of the fishermen's cottages, deep hidden in furzen and bramble patch, brown nets, shining still with silver scales, were hanging up to dry. In one of the gardens crab pots stood in a careless heap near a row of murmuring straw skeps under an over-grown elder hedge. The hedge smelt of nettles in the sun, and fast-sitting hen blackbirds.

Truly it was a legendary sea valley with its stiles built of old oars, with woods gay with butterfly orchids, and with every field thick-spangled with elfin flowers.

How footsore we were as we trudged back along the straight road towards Greenhill Gardens in the Lodmoor twilight, and yet how happy, too, completely innocent of the treasures we were bringing home with us, treasures of the memory to be in our lives more lasting than the material shells and stones that we carried in our hands.

MONTACUTE HOUSE

IN THE YEAR 1931, MONTACUTE HOUSE, ONE OF THE MOST PERFECT examples of an Elizabethan country house in England, was formally taken over by the National Trust and so became a State monument safe from mutilation or destruction. It had been the home of the Phelips family for three hundred and fifty years. A Phelips had built it and a Phelips had sold it. Montacute House is entirely constructed of Ham Hill stone, a golden habitation speaking elegantly enough of the prosperity of the Tudor times, when, under the rule of a headstrong dynasty, a moiety of peace was ensured throughout the land of England, and noblemen and gentry came no longer to consider entrenched and moated castles necessary for their safety.

It was in the year 1886 that my father was offered the living of Montacute by Mr W R Phelips, and when I was two years old we moved from Dorchester to our new home, a large Victorian vicarage.

It was my privilege therefore to witness at close quarters the last years of this Reformation family in their celebrated dwelling. When I recall my childhood I often now feel as if I had lived two lives, one in the eighteenth century and one in the twentieth. Over-looking the moss-grown wall of the rook-haunted, garlic-floored spinney down by the old Montacute Mill I well remember in our nursery walks seeing a noticeboard with the words 'Beware of Man Traps' still clearly legible upon its weather-worn wood.

It has been for three generations the business of my family as country clergymen to stand between the landed gentry and the people of the village. This was an office my father was called upon to perform at Montacute. The Squire was a highly cultured gentleman with a kindly disposition, but the traditions of his class were firmly fixed in him. He never questioned his right to be an autocratic ruler over the lives of all those who lived upon his hereditary acres, and the democratic assertiveness that became common among the working classes toward the latter end of the nineteenth century was constantly resented by him.

In those days there were beggar women to be found in almost every parish. Nancy Cooper, an old witch woman, would come from her hovel in 'the hungry air of Odcombe' to gather sticks in the Montacute Park. The Squire never interfered with the activities of this aged woman. Perhaps he regarded her as part of his feudal estate, like some twisted tree that he would by no means let his woodsman tamper with.

Her daughter Betsy, whose birth had been the cause of her disgrace, was the old beggar woman's constant companion, and now grown to middle life, was little less tattered than was her mother.

This Betsy I came to know well. Once when my brother John and I met her in the Odcombe Street we tried to get her to show us where her mother was buried. She went pathetically stumbling to and fro over the graves with tears rolling down her cheeks, repeating again and again, 'I be so mazed, I be, I didn't mind now where she do lie—she were a blessed mother and no mistake. 'Tis the nights when I do miss she terrible bad—the rats out on boards.'

The Squire's mother must have been about the same age as Nancy Cooper, and yet how different had been the life of this other human female of high rank!

I do not think I have ever seen an old lady with so delicate a complexion. Even in her great age the poise of her head was light and graceful as a rose upon its stalk. The moulding of her skull was as fragile as that of the most precious porcelain and there was a flush upon her cheeks that reminded me of the inside of some of the sea shells in my father's cabinet. Her head was as ethereal in appearance as was Shelley's head, and she was, as a matter of fact, the daughter of Shelley's cousin, and the poet's first love, the same who forsook him to bestow the favours of her beauty upon the wealthy Squire of Coker Court in Somerset.

When old Nancy and her daughter would, with crooked spines, be 'sticking' under the great Montacute sycamores, crooning to each other on the eternal subjects of back and belly, this little light-footed great lady could be seen walking along the drive that ran under the avenue to Galpin's Lodge; unless she had chosen, as she sometimes did, the damp woodland path of Park Cover, a woodland path bordered by a shelving bank thick with mosses out of which in the autumn slippery toadstools of bright scarlet would grow. Who ever knew the long, long thoughts that were revolving in that solitary old woman's head, so aristocratic and so ancient, as she trod the ancestral woods of her husband's family, which, during those mild wet months before Christmas, never ceased from their melancholy dripping?

Her husband, the Squire's father, inherited eighteenth century tastes, and through his love of gaming had so compromised the Phelips estate that it never afterwards recovered. In the hall there is an oil painting of him standing life-size in his park, tall hat in hand, the great house he ruined reduced by perspective to the size of a doll's house.

Near Ilchester there are two farms called Sock and Beerly. These farms at one time rounded off the Phelips property to the north. I used to be told by the country people this story about them. The gambling Squire was staying at Weymouth, and on a wet afternoon, having nothing to do, staked a bet on one of two flies that were crawling up the window-pane. When his friend's fly reached the wooden plinth which marked the winning post of this fantastic circus race, the idle sparks who were watching heard the Master of Montacute mysteriously exclaim, 'There go Sock and Beerly.'

One of my earliest recollections of Mrs. Phelips, senior, is of her driving me and her grandson Gerard, who was my own age, to Yeovil. Arrived in the town, she told the coachman to draw up at the toy-shop which stood opposite 'The Choughs.' On the proprietor's obsequiously hurrying out to the carriage door, he was instructed to give us our choice of all his wares. I

A Phelips family group seated in the alcoves, 1910. (Photo: National Trust)

was so bewildered as I was ushered round the crowded passages of the small shop that I selected a painted tricycle that went by clockwork, afterward envying the cooler judgement of my companion, who brought back for our inspection in the gallery a very expensive, and apparently inexhaustible, conjuring box.

Often we would be invited to a nursery tea with the four Phelips children. We would walk down the long drive on those winter afternoons with our black shining house shoes in a basket, and Miss Beales sedately leading the way. I remember choking at one of those teas and being carried behind the heavy winter curtains so that I might recover from my embarrassment in private, and how, before making my appearance once more at the candle-lighted tea table, I climbed up on the sill to look out of the high window and was amazed to find that in the courtyard below all was as bright as day. In that one glimpse through the small glass panes I received an impression of the enchantment of moonshine that has remained with me all my life—the fountain, the dovecot, the stone flags, the very weeds in their crevices edged with an exact hoarfrost whiteness.

It was Marjorie, the elder of the two Phelips girls, who had put me behind the curtain. She had always protected me since, under my brother John's direction, we had acted *Macbeth* and I had played the part of her little son, the son of Lady Macduff, piping out to her the words 'As birds do, mother.' The squire, I remember, invented a method of imitating the sound of thunder by beating a large sheet of tin with a broom handle, and was amused because, for reasons of temperance, my mother would not agree to having wine served to us at the banquet, but in its stead gave us raspberry vinegar.

The interior of Montacute House stirred my imagination—the armoury for example, with helmets and cuirasses used at the time of the Great Rebellion. Whenever I passed through this high square-shaped room I experienced a kind of *Ivanhoe* romance, and although the Phelips family came into prominence after the Wars of the Roses, echoes from the days of medieval chivalry would be clearly audible to me as I looked up at the weapon-hung walls of the civil antechamber. The main stairway was exciting also, the long stone slabs worn uneven by so much Phelips shoe leather; but most wonderful of all it was to step suddenly into the immense gallery that stretched one hundred and eighty feet from end to end of the house.

How the lonely memories of the old gallery would be scattered, as, with the careless voices of living children, we burst in upon its emptiness; and how hollow, how resonant, its bare boards would sound as our quick feet went pattering, racing down them, unheedful of anything but the impinging actuality of our moment's holiday! How swiftly, too, on a rainy afternoon the time would go by in so spacious a playing room! The great rocking-horse was kept there, the highest-stepping dapple grey ever built by a carpenter, left alone through so many long hours to contemplate with the painted eye the procrastinating twilights of the morning and evening shading their way through sixteen windows, along the coved ceiling of this vast Elizabethan corridor.

The rain would beat against one or other of the high oriel windows at each end of the gallery, where, to the south, the village was overlooked, or where, at the other end, the stately ornamental North Gardens could be seen, with their dark drenched yew trees standing like royal sentinels against the meadows that rose into view beyond the privileged enclosure.

How soon death—impersonal, implacable—removes the fairy-tale characters from the dreams of our lives! Where now is the old Squire, and where now the young Squire, and where the second daughter of the house, whose hair was of the finest golden texture—the hair of a princess in a story-book, as indeed she always seemed, whether leaning from the top of one of the garden walls to pick an apricot sweetened by the summer sun, or in a wide summer hat, seated at the back of one of the Pitt Pond pleasure boats?

I do not think any occurrence I have observed in my life has given me sharper understanding of the insubstantiality of all temporal values than the separation of this house from the Phelipses. How completely for centuries they had dominated the countryside of South Somerset! They sold their hereditary farms and disposed of their hereditary manor with apparent indifference. It had not ever been in their style to wear their hearts upon their sleeves, and the outer world was never permitted to gauge at what emotional cost they were finally divided from the wood and stones and pasture lands that had for so long been theirs in perpetual freehold.

As a boy I used to visit a bed-ridden Montacute labourer. He was so old that to move himself at all he had to lay hands on a rope-end tied to the bottom rail of his rusty bedstead. This old man initiated me into an odd tradition that must have been current for generations in the village. The Phelips crest represents a blazing fire held in an iron cresset, and in years gone by some inventive mind among the commonalty must have suggested the following explanation of the sign. In a far period of antiquity, even before Thomas Phelips possessed himself of 'half a burgage' in the Montacute parish, the rightful heir of the property had been burned to death. The King of England, hearing of the deed, had given orders that the Phelips family should for all times carry the flaming beacon as their sign—'to mind 'em of it for everlasting.'

The crest is familiar to everybody who lives in Montacute, and has been so for centuries. It is placed on each side of the great gates of the west drive and is painted clear for all eyes to see on the swinging tavern board that hangs outside the 'Phelips Arms' at the top of the Borough. Without doubt, the explanation of its meaning communicated to me by old John Hann on his death-bed was the one generally accepted by the apple-orchard labourers and Ham Hill quarrymen with heads besotted with cider. To this day I remember certain of the old man's more dramatic expressions. 'Thik sign on top of they girt posties along by Vicarage do tell o' sommat,' and again, 'My granfer would say, God Almighty will shift 'em for it, may be in thy time, may be in thy childer's time, but sure as day comes he'll unroosty 'em.'

NANCY COOPER

URING CERTAIN PERIODS OF MY LIFE I HAVE BEEN IN DESPAIR about making a living. In San Francisco I remember envying the men who were selling newspapers on the streets, so securely attached did they seem to the ordinary day-to-day economic life of the human race. This feeling of incompetence before an efficient and prosperous world I began to experience very early in my career. When a telegram arrived at Montacute Vicarage announcing that I had been 'ploughed' in the Historical Tripos I well remember setting out upon a long walk by myself in a vain attempt to solve the practical problems brought to a head by my riotous living at Cambridge.

Eventually I entered a tavern at the top of Hendford Hill. Nobody except the landlord was in the place, and I presently began confiding to him my predicament. He listened with grave attention to all I told him, and when I had finished was ready with his answer. He advised me to apply at once for the position of Master of the Yeovil Workhouse which he declared had just fallen vacant. It was a post he said easily accessible to one of my attainments, and would be, so he assured me, 'a bed of roses'. Afterwards, whenever I passed the Yeovil Workhouse, either on foot or sitting by the side of my father in the family trap, I found myself observing the outside of the long, low, substantially constructed building with an interest almost proprietary, the outside of this firm building grown over with Virginia creeper, and representing the complacent solution of the Victorians for the vexed problems connected with eld and pauperism in the neighbouring villages.

At that time there used to come almost daily to our back door a beggar woman named Nancy Cooper. She was very old, and there was something so arresting about her personality that she remains still a living memory in the cottages of Odcombe and Montacute. She and her daughter Betsy Cooper in their sensational patched clouts were perhaps the very last of the long procession of Elizabethan, Caroline, and eighteenth century beggars to remain unmolested by modern poor-law organisation. How this old woman fascinated the imaginations of us children, this Meg Merrilies from Odcombe whom we so continually met on our nursery walks in the lanes and in the Montacute House Park, appearing in her tags as a veritable fairybook figure. I do not suppose the county of Somerset ever possessed a more notable vagrant. Her face was seamed with criss-crossed, crow's-foot lines, her cheeks showing flabby and ashen-white under the old cotton sun-bonnet it was her custom always to wear. Her tattered skirt and petticoats, foul and enfolded, scarcely reached below her knees, and about her legs were wound endless scantlings of material held in position by pieces of thick string after the manner of swineherds and other country folk in Saxon times. Her feet were shod with heavy hob-nailed boots, which, even when the turnpikes were covered with the white dust of summer, permanently retained their encrustation of mud! We children knew nothing of Nancy's past life, though our old cook, Ellen Childs, would sometimes hint darkly, as she stirred the pot, that Nancy presented a crowning example of the way God could correct a wilful life 'when He was so minded'. She used to tell us that she was once as dainty a maid as any in Montacute, and even in her great old age Nancy Cooper's eyes were as blue as the hedgerow periwinkles that grow about the little cottage-well to the right of the road at the bottom of Preston Hill coming out from Yeovil.

The story of Nancy Cooper's life, as I have managed to recover it, possesses a ballad quality that is strangely moving. She was the only daughter of a Montacute man who owned his own cottage and other freehold property. Her mother died when she was a baby and her father when she was still a young girl. As a village heiress she had several suitors, but the lad she idled after was a young ne'er-do-well who was known by the odd nickname of 'Snack'. Nancy's neighbours tried hard to dissuade her from this match and she was so far influenced by their forebodings as to break with the boy the day before the wedding. She was, however, a passionate girl, the boy was her choice, and she could not rid her mind of her infatuation. He continued to play upon her feelings and they were eventually married. Within the space of two years 'Snack' had squandered all Nancy's property and had sailed for Canada, leaving her with a baby at the breast. The Montacute people were sorry for her and did what they could to help her, but times were difficult during the first half of the nineteenth century, and it was impossible for them to continue their support. Nancy Cooper had not been brought up to work for her bread, and was perhaps unable fully to appreciate the sacrifices that were being made for her. She was too proud, 'too independent' as they say in the country, to go into the Yeovil Workhouse, so she had no other choice than to begin her vagabond life. With her baby in her arms she tramped the lanes, sleeping where she could, in sheds sometimes, sometimes in hedge-shelters, and sometimes in the open fields.

There was at that time living in Montacute a quarryman named Tom Richards. He was a heavy drinker, an honest, good-natured, trusty fellow, 'as jocund as a tun'. He was a native of the nearby village of Stoke-sub-Hamdon, and was 'a character', stories about his eccentricities being still current in the village. There used to be the remains of an old lime kiln at the top of the field called Witcombe, not far from the road that runs from Odcombe to Ham Hill, a road which during the eighteenth century served as the main coaching highway between London and Exeter. This kiln in those days was in full working order and a lean-to shed had been built by it so that the lime burners could be sheltered in bad weather. Tom Richards formed the habit of sleeping in the shed when he had taken 'a drop too much' at the 'Prince of Wales', lying snug on a bed of straw with his jolly head against a bag of lime. Often he would make the men laugh by his comical way of singing an old Crimean war song.

Cottage in Wash Lane, Montacute believed to be Nancy Cooper's.   (Photo: Alan Clark)

As a matter of fact, he only knew two lines of the famous Balaclava ditty, and these he shamelessly misused, bawling out, so that his voice might have disturbed the rooks roosting on Miles Hill, the last word—Roar.

The big guns they did rattle
The small guns they did ROAR.

Tom Richards had come through the 'hungry forties', and when the shadow of the approaching winter lay across the village with work scarce on the hill, he would console the faint-hearted by saying, as with no 'heel-taps' he whiffed up the contents of his mug: 'If us da starve theas winter ta be the first time.'

This happy-go-lucky quarry-man, as 'drunk as a mouse', was returning to Montacute one late evening through Stoke Wood. As he came by a splendid old beech tree which used to stand to the left of the path—a tree whose white enwrapping bark resembled a palimpsest so many were the names of the lovers that had been carved on it—he fancied he heard some sound amongst the leaves high in the wood to his right. Curious to know what it was, he made his way up the slippery slope, and to his amazement came upon Nancy occupied in scraping out a primitive pit-shelter for herself and her baby. The kind-hearted labourer begged her not to think of sleeping in such a place, and offered her the freedom of his own cottage. Nancy, however, would not agree to this. 'Then', said Tom, 'you shan't bide here aloan all night. If you won't come wi I, I shall bide here along be you.' It was thus that their love began on a midsummer's night in Hedgecock.

> *'Harp and carp, Thomas,' she said,*
> *'Harp and carp along wi' me;*
> *And if ye dare to kiss my lips*
> *Sure of your bodie I will be.'*

The pair became inseparable after those hours spent together in the greenwood, and it was not long before Nancy consented to become the mistress of his cottage. This cottage has since been pulled down, but I have been told it used to stand in the little garden that may now be seen on the right hand of Wash Lane where it branches out of Middlestreet in Montacute. Nancy proved herself a good and faithful partner to Tom Richards, and the two were as happy as a pair of jackdaws. They had several children. Disaster, however, is never far away from the poor. Tom Richards as he grew older fell sick, and though Nancy nursed him as best she could their narrow resources soon became exhausted. It was useless for the little household to apply for outdoor relief, as in those stern days the guardians of the poor would never have consented to expend public money on the welfare of an adulterous couple. In desperation Nancy Cooper allowed him to be taken from her and put into the Workhouse Infirmary; she herself, meanwhile, like any sturdy baggage of medieval times, resuming her former outlawry. She was never permitted to see him again. He lingered for some time and then died. As a pauper his corpse had to be returned for burial in his original parish of Stoke-under-Ham. When the morning of the funeral arrived Nancy was seen walking backwards and forwards below the Workhouse wall. She was wearing an old grey hat in the place of her sun-bonnet, and her hob-nailed boots had been polished as black as pitch. The vehicle containing the coffin emerged at last from the Workhouse drive and the pathetic *cortège*, with its single mourner weeping behind, began to pass through the village of Preston at an orderly pace. When the hearse reached the bottom of Preston Hill where the periwinkles grow, the men, wishing to get on with their work, urged the horse into a trot. To keep up Nancy had now to run behind the conveyance like the dog we used to see faithfully running behind the baker's cart. When the Lufton turning was reached she could keep it up no longer, and allowed the vehicle to draw away from her. Sometimes running, sometimes walking, the distracted woman hurried after the disappearing carriage. When she passed through the Montacute streets she was dripping with sweat. In spite of their assumed attitude of stolid indifference village people have a peculiar genius for seizing upon any salient fact that emphasises the dramatic in life; in the present instance they did not fail to remark that Nancy, in her pitiful race across the Borough, passed close by her husband, 'Snack', who, having long since returned from Canada, was idling outside the Phelips Arms.

The Borough, Yeovil, as Llewelyn Powys knew it in 1900. (Photo: Somerset Rural Life Museum)

When Nancy reached Stoke the service was over, the clergyman gone, and the grave was being hastily filled in by two grave-diggers. As soon as they had finished their task these men shouldered their tools, informing Nancy that she must now leave as they had to lock the gates. At these words she threw herself upon the new mound with a passion so violent that the attention of the men was arrested. They used to tell how she drew out of the folds of her rags bright-coloured hedgerow leaves, strewing them over the turfless grave and crooning to herself between choking sobs—'Poor Tom, poor Tom.'

At the end of the century it was a common thing to see a group of village boys gathered about Nancy Cooper. For a few coppers the aged woman would dance a grotesque jig of her own invention, lifting up her huge boots in simulated mirth and chanting in a toneless voice over and over again the one line she could remember of an old song.

Jolly fat farmers all in a row!
Jolly fat farmers all in a row!
Jolly fat farmers all in a row!
Jolly fat farmers all in a row!
Jolly fat farmers all in a row!

My mother could never bear to be told of these pitiful performances, but the children of Bishopston and Middlestreet would at any moment leave their marbles in order to witness with shouts of laughter the uncouth spectacle.

When Nancy died, Betsy, her daughter, continued to live the same vagrant life. She would come to our back-door nearly every day, and I would often call her up to the little platform outside the saddle-room where I had had a couch placed and was trying to cure myself of consumption. Her imaginative forms of speech, so penetrated with a native hedge-and-ditch lore, a speech often instinct with poetry, a speech Shakespearean in its directness, and in no way similar to the canting expressions of ordinary beggars, always held my interest.

On my return from Africa after the war I made inquiries about Betsy, and was told by Dr Hensleigh Walter, the sympathetic physician of the district, that the authorities in their mania for external parochial orderliness had had Betsy evicted from her Odcombe hovel and sent to the Yeovil Workhouse. Betsy, confined in the strict, official building, fretted her heart out, like a caged moor-hen. In a few weeks she had died from a kind of claustrophobia.

EXMOOR

WHEN I WAS LIVING AT WHITE NOSE I RECEIVED A LETTER FROM a small coal merchant in Dorchester offering to sell me a load of peat, and before many days I had a good stack of this excellent fuel in my backyard. It is likely that never before had peat been burned on the famous chalk headland. On late frosty afternoons, when the wind was blowing from the north, and the hare 'limp'd trembling through the frozen grass', the gipsy-like aroma of burning turf would come to me upon the fresh inland air. It was a rough incense evocative of far-away memories.

When I was fifteen years old my brother Littleton, who was ten years my senior, planned that we should spend a fortnight fly-fishing on Exmoor. He provided me with a rod, and used to stand by me for hours on the Montacute lawn teaching me how to throw a fly. Up to that time my only experience of the sport had been bottom-fishing in Pitt Pond. I would be content to sit by the edge of that large woodland tarn, angling in dark waters, my eyes fixed upon my coloured float, hoping and hoping to see it quiver and be carried, a moment afterwards, resolutely out of sight. I had never been to Exmoor before, and it was an adventure that influenced my whole life. We arrived at Minehead with the April sunshine splashing down on the pavements, and with daffodils in flower in every garden. A farm-cart was at the station waiting to convey us to Malmsmead; the driver was a young man who spoke with a broad Devonshire accent, his 'twoos' sounding to my ears like a foreign language.

It was nearly five o'clock in the afternoon before we reached the top of Porlock Hill. It was one of those spring evenings that seem as cool as a mossy grotto, when all life appears suddenly wide awake like a little girl talking to herself in her nursery cot. The landlord of the Ship Inn stepped brisk and gay along his narrow office-passage, now no longer darkened by doors closed against winds and sleet. Boys were out in the dewy lanes playing and calling, and the first petals of flowers were beginning to fall upon the first white dust. My mood as I rested by my brother's side on the top of Porlock Hill was one of utter happiness. Lying in the heather, I had in my mind no vision of the place to which the cart, not yet to be seen at the crest of the steep road, was about to carry us; I only was aware that the evening sky seemed wider in its circumference than I had ever known it in South Somerset, extending its celestial hoop far off over the wild enfolded hills, and far over a broad sea of speedwell blue, emphatic of life's fortunate freedoms.

We reached the farm at twilight. While our evening meal was preparing I had time to run out and stand on the bridge to watch the trout poised in the clean water below. Day and night the sound of the river was audible in

Minehead Station. 'A farm cart was at the station waiting to convey us to Malmsmead.'

John Ridd's farm. In the afternoons when the baker called, energetic and with no time for thoughts other than those connected with his business, the unending melody continued, and when I waked in the small hours, curled up beside my brother on a huge feather bed, I would hear it still, this music utterly unfamiliar to my ears, different altogether from the regular breaking of the waves on Weymouth Beach, different from the sound of the rain driving against the leaves of the trees in a summer garden. It was as though we lay during those nights dreaming in the bowl

Porlock. Ship Inn.

of a huge silver bell, a bell that was always and always ringing for the festival of life, with a tune as simple and incessant as that which comes from the banded neck of a bell-wether browsing amongst thyme and devil's-bit.

That first evening meal in the old farm I have never forgotten. A deep dish of Devonshire cream, and a loaf of brown bread with lightly boiled fresh eggs, were set before us on a lamp-lit, tea-laid table in a room smelling of the peat fire glowing red on the open hearth; indeed, the smell of burning peat permeated the whole room—the curtains smelt of it, the Devonshire cream tasted of it!

Perhaps it was the lack of any conspicuous success with my rod that made me persuade my brother—a born fisherman, he is always happiest on the bank of a river—to sacrifice his birthday for a walk to Dunkery Beacon. We set out up Badgery Water on a morning of sunshine, our pockets stuffed with provisions. Side by side we walked over wide stretches of burned heather, the charred, twisted twigs of which kept loosening the laces of my boots. In after years when I rode across land in Africa devastated by a bush fire it was always to the fells around Dunkery Beacon that my dreams would go, as, rendered stupid by the sun, I dozed in the saddle while my white Somali pony, with ever-blackening fetlocks, made his way over the vast waste.

At certain seasons we often hear the piping of curlews as they fly across Chaldon Down on their way to the seashore, but it was on this April walk across Exmoor that for the first time I listened to their wild voices. We had sat down on some tussocks at the foot of Dunkery Beacon and must have disturbed one of the birds, for round and round us it flew, often near enough for its long curved bill to be clearly visible. In nature if any sound

Dunkery Beacon through the doorway of Selworthy Church. 'In after years, when I rode across land in Africa devastated by a bush fire, it was always to the burned heather of the fells around Dunkery Beacon that my dreams would go.' (Photo: Alfred Vowles)

is burdened with romance it is the curlew's call. Don Quixote on two separate occasions explained to Sancho Panza how King Arthur at his death was transformed into a crow, and truly, when we hear the dolorous crying of a curlew far up in the heavens, it is not difficult to imagine that we are listening to the bird spirit of a king wailing for the fair dust of a paramour dead long centuries ago.

From Dunkery Beacon we dropped down through the Horner Woods, and it was then to my great delight that we saw red deer. That civil people can still be found willing to hunt to death these proud beasts is to me extraordinary. It is indeed a striking example of how the sanctions of the unimaginative conventional world can obscure, even for intelligent people, the higher values of life. Who can say whether a warrantable stag is less sensitive or less highly developed than a stabled horse? Even Thomas Bewick, always rough and ready, noticed their eyes as being 'peculiarly beautiful, soft, and sparkling.' Surely the laughing girls who every August gather at Cloutsham Farm to kill so god-like an animal, as it were for a game, must have hidden their hearts at the breaking of the cold summer's dawn in the grey water of Watchet or Bridgwater Bay!

> *All that is deathless of me I have laid*
> *In a crystal box on the magic sea,*
> *With the currents of stars and the winds of space*
> *It is drifting away in eternity.*

Let us dismiss from our minds such sorrowful controversies and return to the cliffs of Dorset, where even the foxes 'wise in counsel' are left unmolested. Often at White Nose I have lain flat upon a fresh-ploughed furrow in order that I might smell the very body of the earth, and on those occasions when the seaside air carried upon its gusts the tang of my peat fire it would seem to me that I was inhaling also the earth's light breath. Through the mysterious power of such simple sacramental experiences it becomes more easy in old age, or in sickness, for a lover of life to borrow with resignation the octogenarian's apostrophe to the earth in the *Canterbury Tales:*

> *'I knokke with my staf, erly and late.*
> *And saye "Deare Moder let me in." '*

HAM HILL

THE IMPORTANCE OF A HILL AS A LANDMARK IN A DISTRICT CAN by no means be always measured by its elevation. Ham Hill is a good example of this. Despite its modest proportions it is an eminence remarkably conspicuous from all directions. Men harvesting in the rich arable lands of Taunton Vale look across at it. 'Drowners' employed in cutting osiers in the dykes of Sedgemoor watch its outline for weather portents. It is clearly visible from the eastern foothills of the Quantocks, and shepherds on the Mendips and Corton Beacon have from their childhood been familiar with its shape, as it were the shape of a couchant lion which for centuries has lain perfectly motionless against the horizon, the vigilant warden of the wide water-meadows of the west.

To account for the apparently inexhaustible supply of stone that the hill has always provided, the old women of Montacute used to assure my father with the utmost gravity that the stone 'grew', and when one considers the number of the abbeys, churches, manor houses, farms, cow sheds, pounds, bridges, field walls, scullery floors, and milestones which once lay raw in the bowels of this yellow mountain this belief appears almost plausible. I have often wondered out of which particular quarry of Ham Hill the stones that form the fan tracery of the roof of Sherborne Abbey were lifted—perhaps from the same bed that was destined to provide flagstones for the notorious Ilchester gaol, stones of devotion and stones of despair deriving from a single matrix of unimplicated nature!

The late Mr W B Wildman, the old fifth form master at Sherborne, whose wide Rabelaisian imagination awakened the intelligences of so long a procession of English school boys, enlivening the dullest lesson with a characteristic mixture of wit and learning, would often make reference to the amphitheatre at the northern end of Ham Hill, thereby bringing vividly before the minds of his pupils the period of the Roman occupation. In graphic language he would describe how some wretched subject Briton would be dragged to this diminutive arena to make a soldier's holiday, either by fighting against another of his race, or against some wild beast imported from a far distant jungle. On such occasions I would listen to his words with all the lively personal attention natural to a boy who hears allusions made to a locality familiar to his holiday life. As I grew older I would often examine the mole hills around the amphitheatre, and I found the flat muscular hands of those little gentlemen in velvet were in the habit of unwittingly casting up scraps of Roman pottery in their sedulous sub-terranean tunnelling after earth-worms. On these wide northern levels of the hill, covered so smoothly with turf, sheep find the best grazing in the county. We used to come here to discover whether the floods were out. What a sight they were after a period of heavy rain, a wide sheet of white water covering half the county, stretching away past Athelney and Bridgwater to the western sea! And how rewarding to walk on Ham Hill on a fine spring day when the fields of Longload and High Ham lie prosperously awaiting the return of another summer; when the daisy paddocks immediately below are patched with the drying amber-coloured skins of the gloving factories; when dandelions are out everywhere in the roadside hedges; and the songs of larks are so loud that they all but drown the scrannel pipings of the little Hebditch shepherd boy. Then at last the night takes possession of the hill under the wide-spread silence of the stars, with aromatic winds blowing gently up over the ancient vallums from the distant hayfields of Wullam's Mill. Forty years have so entirely altered the manner of our living that it has become no easy matter to envisage the life of Ham Hill as it was during the last quarter of Queen Victoria's reign, with rumbling carts bringing down skilfully moulded blocks cradled on beds of bracken, and with ill-paid men in dusty yellow-powdered breeches—in breeches of gold ('Stoke roughs', as the less generous landed gentry did not hesitate to call them) at the head of the horses, everyone of them hearty Sunday night drinkers and stout voters for Strachey. What toil those Ham Hill horses, with their defeated tragic heads, used to endure hauling waggons up the steep ways in the dust of summer and the mud of winter, and then coming down again with perilously heavy loads, skid pans on wheels, but even so with the old carts dangerously jolting and liable to get out of control.

Ham Hill was always a favourite place for political demonstrations. It was here that George Mitchell, the man from the plough, Montacute born and Montacute bred, used to hold his big meetings every Whitsun Monday, hiring no less than seven brass bands to help Joe Arch in his fight for the franchise of the agricultural labourer. He would arrive in a horse-brake with his mother sitting next to the driver, with a placard before her on which the words GO ON were inscribed in large type, and another behind her with the words COME ON enormously displayed. However, in spite of all his hearty good nature and energy and sense of publicity, Mr Mitchell was never able to get himself nominated for Parliament, and at the beginning of the century he died in London in poor circumstances a disappointed man.

The Frying Pan end of Ham Hill is the popular end, but my own preference has always been for the south-western end. This is where the spirit of the ancient hill has been least disturbed. The whole sloping section that lies between Jack O'Beards and Tinker's Spring offers a wayfarer a wonderful prospect of rural peace. It is easy to understand how the finer spirits of the neighbourhood have taken to the civilized and honourable employment of apple growing, tending their Tom Puts, Horners, Leather Jackets, and Pippins under clouds as grey as the feathers of a wood pigeon's breast, clouds scarcely distinguishable from the blue mists that from morning to evening in the autumnal haze obscure the course of the River Parrett as it idly meanders through one fat meadow after the other of the most fertile valley in the West of England.

PITT POND

THE OLD COACH-ROAD FROM LONDON TO EXETER AT ONE TIME ran through the village of Odcombe and from there over Ham Hill. A little past the cross-roads named Five Ashes there still may be seen standing on the bank, half-hidden in grass and bracken, a weather-worn mile-stone with the exact distance between Hyde Park Corner and the sandy Somerset highway, cut deep into its surface. If a traveller walks westward a few hundred yards from this stone, he will observe a gate on his left which leads down to Pitt Pond. This miniature lake was made by one of the Phelipses of Montacute House during the eighteenth century at a time when landscape gardening on a large scale was a fashionable occupation with country gentlemen. Mrs Ingilby has told me that the pond owes its name to the fact that it was William Pitt, the elder, who first put the notion of damming up the stream that runs through the wood into her ancestor's head. It is likely enough that the Great Commoner had come over from his newly acquired property of Burton Pynsent to visit his neighbour, his mind full of the changes that he himself was making on his Sedgemoor hillside, and eager to share with any friend the advantages of his own lively invention.

As I remember Pitt Pond there was little about it to suggest the artifice of the Georgian period. In the passing of nearly two centuries it had gathered to itself a singular atmosphere, an atmosphere at once melancholy and romantic. In the sodden days of November, when the dampness of the Montacute meadows penetrated to the very marrow bones of man and beast, and the woods were all enshrouded in mist, and the deep, sandy lanes became dim tunnels in which the wheels of carts sank up to their axles, the breath of Pitt Pond was as the absolute breath of mortality, the breath of a universal mortality which comprehended birds, fishes, reptiles, and the lowest forms of life in the vegetable world. To visit Pitt Pond during this month was in the old days like visiting one of those dark tarns of Edgar Allan Poe's lurid imaginings. As soon as ever the great white woodland gate opposite Horses Covert had been squeezed through by us children, the swing of its hinges being heavily impeded by the gross mud, we would inhale an afflatus of putrescence such as would be inconceivable to anyone who had not been accustomed to dwelling upon the sullen deposits of Somerset's deepest clay.

In hard January weather all this would be different. It is true that, as we raced along the laurel-bordered track that led from the white gate to the pond, we would still pass through toad-stool-smelling atmospheres; but the frost would have completely transformed the sylvan lake. The surrounding trees would fret the sky with branches naked and salubrious. The fir trees about the boat-house would stand out darkly, giving to that corner of the pond a scarcely definable Santa Claus look, or perhaps a

Russian look, as they lifted their cold spears to the clouds, their roots, snake-like, often protruding sheer out of the black ice. For both at its deep and its shallow end the ice of Pitt Pond was as smooth as whale-bone and as black as gun-metal. When with the help of a gimlet borrowed from our father's tool-box we had screwed on to our boot heels our old-fashioned skates, fastening their leather straps about our toes, how gaily we would glide away from the rushy, frosty-white bank towards 'the island', which, built of Ham Hill stones piled together, stood round and solid at the pond's centre! We would often continue skating till darkness began to fall, when, under the contracting compulsion of the increased cold, the ice would become more and more resonant, emitting alarming, unexplained, booming sounds that knocked and groaned and echoed mysteriously from one dark margin to another.

Mr Wyndham Goodden, the eldest son of the Vicar of Montacute who was my father's immediate predecessor, told me a happy story concerning an occasion when he and a boy named Donne, who came from Odcombe, stayed skating by moonlight at Pitt Pond till a late hour. Mr and Mrs Goodden in great anxiety because their son had not returned for either tea or dinner sent Crago, the gardener, up to Pitt to look for him. When at last the truant came in at the front door of his home 'as hungry as a hunter' he was met in the first hall by his father, who, in his autocratic, grave way, insisted that his dare-devil boy, still glowing from his recent exercise and charged with youth's sanguine temper, should come with him into his study to offer up a prayer of thanks 'to Almighty God' for a safe return.

Pitt Pond has been the scene of more than one tragedy. It was here that a man named Hann, the parent of a nursemaid of ours, drowned himself one early morning. The lonely reservoir had without doubt a kind of autumnal affinity with death which might very well appeal to a deranged mind hag-ridden by despair.

In the summer all was altered. Then the great woodland pool lay engulfed in an ocean of leaves. To the north the tree-tops were so close mingled as to form a solid slope of embossed green only slightly darker than the grass of Pitt Plain. At the fountainhead of the little stream that filled the pond was the Montacute House water-cress-bed, so fresh and virginal in the cuckoo-calling tortoise-shell-butterfly April mornings, that it might well have been a grazing ground frequented by the legendary white hart of the Blackmore Vale in the cold sacred hour of the dawn! It was in the summer time that we would on occasions be invited to a picnic in the ruined keeper's cottage which stood at the pond's north-east corner. The pleasure boats would be brought out of their dark house into the sunshine and Mr Phelips, after the manner of a highly endowed benevolent mandarin, would pleasure himself with the guileless occupation of rowing silently absorbed children over his fish-filled water—for Pitt Pond was always packed with roach, which, together with large lusty fat eels, seemed to thrive on the nourishment produced by the leechy mud at the bottom of the forest mere.

It was at Pitt Pond that I learned first to fish. Though in later years I have sometimes felt uneasy about the moral propriety of this diversion, in those thoughtless days such misgivings were far from my mind. I exulted in every one of the processes that had to do with the treacherous pastime. I marvelled at the fact that a few minutes after mustard-water had been poured between its stone slabs the backyard would be alive with worms ready to be picked up and placed in an empty cocoa tin as bait. The ingenious method of mixing dough with cotton wool that it might hold to the hook the better, excited my admiration; as also did the look of the dainty hooks themselves, so deftly barbed; and the hair thread, with its tiny weights of slit shot, almost invisible at the end of a rod elongated to a surprising length by its neatly fitting sections. What an intensity of suspended excitement used to take possession of me, as I sat at the deep-end near the sluice, watching the brightly painted float, till at last, after a few tentative bobs, it would suddenly disappear. I would jump to my feet and in a moment a red-finned roach would be flicking its taut electric body to and fro in the tangled grass. With fingers smelling of water-mint and fish-scales I would remove the merciless steel from the creature's throat, leaving it with its detached staring eyes and spasmodic leaps to gasp away its life in its basket-bed of earth-fragrant moss.

I have never visited Pitt Pond since the Montacute estate was sold. The trees of the woods after this sad event took place were delivered into the hands of lumber-men, and the 'unprofitable' pond, no longer valued, has been allowed to relapse into its natural state. In due course the stone-built dam at the deep end, responsible for holding in the water, gave way, and at present, I am told, there is only a muddy morass over-grown with reeds surrounding a central heap of stones. Through this morass a small woodland stream slowly meanders between soft damp banks of mud which are occasionally, when the weather has been exceptionally cold, marked with the chalk of a migratory woodcock.

TINTINHULL

THE OTHER DAY AS I RESTED ON MY BALCONY LOOKING OUT AT the mountains of Switzerland glittering bright in the frosty sunshine the postman arrived with a parcel from England. It contained a photograph of the stocks under the old elm at Tintinhull which a young girl, living beneath the shadow of Ham Hill, had thought might be of interest to me. She had judged rightly for the faded picture revived in my mind I know not how many memories.

Tintinhull is situated scarcely two miles distant from my old home at Montacute, and the village, lying as it does, between the Fosse Way and the road from Yeovil, still remains relatively untroubled by the rude invasion of modern traffic. I have visited it at all hours and in all seasons. I have visited it on cold December mornings when there was a sprinkling of Jack Frost on the backs of each one of Farmer Mead's sheep, and cat-ice about everywhere on the roads, and when the mighty hammer-strokes of Blacksmith Allen and his sons would sound through the clear air as far as Kiss-me-down Covert; and again I have visited it on sultry July noon-tides when the very ducks on the small village pond were too drowsy even so much as to dabble for their lowly viands. My brother John and I used to like to walk there in the Easter holidays after tea. It was a fancy of ours that in no other one of the neighbouring villages did the April evenings fall with so charmed a grace upon leaf and grass and tile and thatch. We never wearied of the scene presented by Tintinhull in the twilight hour, with old sun-bonnet women crossing to the Lamb Inn to fetch cider for their suppers, with tittering gloving girls idling after boys with cowslips stuck in their caps, and with the voices of children floating on the soft Somerset air, on the soft spring air that seemed to smell of opening lilac buds in unseen gardens, and of ground ivy banks, and of the warmed feathers of little hedgerow wild birds.

Tintinhull, or Tyncnell as it was formerly called, is a village redolent of the past. Traces of the 'balks', which once divided the strips of land of the medieval tillage system, may yet be seen in its surrounding fields. The church was originally an Early English one and there is still to be noticed in the chancel a remarkable double piscina of that period. The porch of the church is also notable, with its ribbed roof and ancient nail-studded door, through which so many men and women have passed to and from worship, generation after generation.

How old, how very old the churchyard seems! It is scarce possible to imagine a more suitable place for young people to come to who wish to gain instruction as to the transitory nature of human life. Anybody who loiters in this plot of ground, overlooked by the windows of the old Rectory (now called the Court House) requires no homily from the antic sundial above the porch as to the ordained terms of our existence. There are new gravestones, and old gravestones, and altar-tombs ruined by time, in this

Tintinhull House; the West Front from the Fountain Garden.   (Photo: National Trust)

acre of memories. Very clearly they show that death, even in so sheltered a parish, seldom leaves the sod undisturbed. In June the mounds may lie bland and the churchyard sward unbroken, with bees carrying their honey bags over swaying grasses, with hayfields being mown on every side, and man and beast and fly content in the sweltering work-a-day sunshine; but behold, if visited again before Saint Swithun's, another newly turfed grave is sure to be seen conspicuously and pathetically adorned with Madonna lilies from some mid-summer cottage garden, bereft now and untended.

The village of Tintinhull is especially distinguished for the number of grassy lanes that abound in its neighbourhood. The old road that once ran between Montacute and Ilchester may still be traced out of Montacute as far as the Mill, and from there to Windmill, and so on to Kiss-me-down Covert. From this lovely spinney—Badgeowljay wood as my brother John named it—it crosses the Yeovil road to become a grass-grown halter-path, so unfrequented that it is difficult to believe that it ever represented a main trackway of the district.

There is also a lane below the churchyard wall that leads into a lovely green grove that passes between rich pastures in the direction of Carte Gate. Whenever I see dog-roses my mind is immediately carried back to this happy rural thorough-fare. I have been there when the hedges on both sides were garlanded with these delicate flowers, to be looked upon only perhaps by the preoccupied bright eyes of a predatory magpie, the hungry eyes of a snatch-as-snatch-can gypsy pad-nag, or by the blinking eyes of some drowsy dairy-man-Dick hurrying through the dew of dawn after his cows, his heavy boots not even yet laced up.

To the right of the Dower House opposite the Churchyard wall, there is yet another lane. This lane leads past the Queen Anne Manor eastward to the free fields. When I was a young man this unpretentious but beautiful dwelling house was owned by a highly endowed Doctor of Divinity and although even in those days I felt myself remote from theological controversies I found it a pleasant enough privilege to walk and talk with Doctor Price in his sheltered garden. Doctor Price was sacerdotal to his finger tips. He was an exceptional man, small and frail in appearance, but possessed of a Spartan spirit. Even his wan sensitive smile, for all its charm and urbanity, was never able to conceal the passionate partisanship that he felt for the cause of the clerical faction of his allegiance.

Of all his garden simples he loved none better than his rue, and this romantic herb of grace grew freely along the borders of his protected paths of Ham Hill stone, yellow in the sunlight. Many a time have I sat with him and tried, as he deftly poured out tea from his silver teapot, to follow the intricate workings of his subtle mind. On these occasions I used to observe with refreshment the valerian, wilful and free, that topped the wall overlooking the lane. "Kiss-me-quick", my father has told me, is the correct country name for this lovely flower.

CHILDHOOD MEMORIES

SOME YEARS AGO I LEFT MY COTTAGE ON CHALDON DOWN TO SPEND a few weeks at Weymouth at Brunswick Terrace. It was a time when I was not strong, and I would lie in my room by the open bow window listening to the waves at short regular intervals rattle against the banks of shingle outside; and follow with idle mind each up-and-down of the familiar cliffs, green and white, of the bay that stretched on and on towards St Alban's Head.

For some days my most enterprising adventure was to walk along the quiet pavement in front of the houses, observing with a narrow interest the little April gardens, each with its own separate individuality, that flourished so gaily beneath the dining-room windows of that happy row of holiday lodgings. As I began to get better I became more ambitious and a desire took possession of me to see again the Backwater.

In this mood I remembered the old-fashioned Bath chairs of my childhood, and I at once made inquiries as to the possibility of hiring one of these sedate vehicles out of the past. Duly it arrived at my door, the most perfect Bath chair, more perfect that I could ever have thought possible, soft-cushioned with rose-patterned upholstery such as could only have been favoured in the comfortable years of Victorian middle-class prosperity. The attendant, Mr Hill, with his decorous bearing and independent character, unmistakably belonged to the same great age, and as we talked together I soon discovered that he and I had a deal more in common than general memories of an enviable historic period so fast fading into a remote distance.

Twice a week, when I was at Sherborne Preparatory School under Mr W H Blake, we boys received lessons in copybook writing from Mr Pooley, the schoolmaster of the town, and it was, so we discovered, this same kindly, grey-bearded gentleman who had given instructions to Mr Hill in the difficult art of forming 'pot-hooks'. As a young man Mr Hill had been a servant in one of the Out-Houses of Sherborne School.

We did not on that April afternoon take a direct way to the Backwater for the notion had entered my head to have a look, first of all, at the Alexandra Gardens. These pleasure grounds appeared gay enough to my eyes, warmed by the primrose sunshine which poured down upon the newly mown grass and upon the nodding daffodil trumpets, and upon the pale statuary that stood so lifeless upon their pedestals.

The celebrated Weymouth lagoon, known as the Backwater, had for me many associations. When as children we were taken to Weymouth it was always an important question whether it was wiser to find a window-seat on the right or on the left side of the railway carriage. Looking towards the east it was possible to catch fleeting glimpses of the sea and of White Nose across Lodmoor, whereas looking westward there would be presented a nearer and more prolonged view of the Backwater, with its rushy islands, and hungry fish-eating birds, and snow-white swans against green distant fields. There was more mud about its margins than cement. Its flood-stakes served as fishing stations for cormorants, for cormorants that came flying each morning across the bay from their roosting places on Bats Head or on the Fountain Rock. All was wild and uncared for. In the chill twilight of the seaside dawn the splash of an otter could often be heard, along with the first calling of the cuckoo sounding from Horshoe Copse like a 'haunted bell', or the first song of a lark, clear and tremulous as it rose to the heavens, its neat mottled feather and tiny crest not yet rid of the dew off the Radipole meadows.

In those days the Backwater was rank, sanitary, and beautiful, no attempt having been as yet made to transform it into the tidy, salubrious, and efficiently developed suburb of a prosperous town that wishes to prepare easy promenading for men and women who like to look upon nature, if they look upon it at all, dry shod and from a distance. It is true that now, from the security of my Bath chair, I was in a position to watch the swans at closer range than on former times, to observe their unseemly scramble for food, with serpentine necks adapted to the novel gregarious conditions of snatch-as-snatch-can, as indifferent to the rights of coots as if they were nothing, as if they had not been as especially created as themselves, each little head marked with white as though by the scrupulous application of the Almighty's thumb.

We returned by the back streets and I was soon to be more than ever reminded of the past. During the summer of 1893 we had all been ill of the scarlet fever and when we had recovered it was thought expedient to send us to Weymouth for a change of air. Lodgings were found for us in Invicta House, a new house that faced upon a square at the bottom of the street falling steeply down from Waterloo Place. I was hardly able to recognise the neighbourhood, or indeed Invicta House, so clearly had the passing of forty years altered the plan of the district and mellowed the appearance of the red brick building. Invicta House then belonged to, or at any rate was under the direction of, Mr and Mrs Bowles, kindly people who took a great liking to our nurse Emily and did all that was in their power to make our stay under their roof a happy one.

On one occasion I remember their arranging a magic lantern show for us in their parlour, and something of the excitement of the entertainment remains with me still when I think of my happy suspense as I sat on a chair in the carefully dimmed room next to a friendly and interested neighbour who had also been invited; and the eagerness I felt when the room was once more illumined and trays of sugar biscuits were handed round, together with glasses of the best brew of raspberry vinegar that ever I have drunk in my life. Mr Bowles was not only an expert exponent of the possibilities of the magic lantern, he was also an enthusiastic football player and I well remember being taken to see him perform on some ground on the further side of the Backwater. With my sister Lucy in a perambulator our little troop had eventually made its appearance on the playing field.

We left before the game ended, a chance that caused us to witness one of those incidents of violence so terrifying to imaginative children. A soldier in the old-fashioned red coat of his time came running headlong down the lane with an infuriated mob after him. A few yards from us he was overtaken and fell heavily to the ground from a blow on his back. We hurried on at top speed, but the recollection of that first glimpse of the animal ferocity of man had a profound influence on me, and indeed may have implanted in my mind a deep distrust of every programme of social amelioration that relies upon, or condones, periods of lawlessness for the attainment of Utopian ends.

Yet in those days I was surely no pacifist. Evening after evening I used to sit at the window of Invicta House watching Weymouth boys of my own age playing at soldiers in the square. Perhaps if I had dared to run out to them I would have been welcomed. I did not know. They certainly enjoyed themselves. How shrill their voices used to come to me in the stillness of those late autumn evenings!

> *Such, such were the joys*
> *When we all, girls and boys,*
> *In our youth time were seen*
> *On the Echoing Green.*

I suppose they are now men of fifty, solid townsmen, readers of the *Dorset Daily Echo,* themselves with grown-up children, and may not even remember the gleaming swords they once owned, swords that seemed to me then far more romantic than any real weapon, though it should be old as the dagger recently dredged up from the bottom of the Backwater, from the bottom of that silent floor that has scarcely for thousands of years been disturbed by anything more ruthless than the sliding abdomens of sulky eels resolutely concentrated upon their own hungry quests through fathom-deep water to which no sunlight ever penetrates.

MONTACUTE HILL

Sweet Michael's loveliest of the hills around,
With beauty clad with constant verdure crowned
Beneath thy shade (with name from thee derived)
Sweet Montacute, through numerous years has thrived.

Thomas Shoel

FEW LANDMARKS IN SOUTH SOMERSET ARE MORE CONSPICUOUS than is that of St Michael's Mount under which lies the old-world village of Montacute. The hill rises immediately behind the parish church and the Abbey and overlooks Middlestreet, Bishopston, and the Borough, and indeed each cottage garden, however secluded, of the lovely hamlet. 'After the Hill of Senlac and the vanished choir of Waltham we may fairly place the wooded hill of Montacute,' wrote the historian Freeman. Small wonder therefore that Thomas Shoel, the poet, was so passionately fond of the hill and is rumoured to have sat for hours upon its crest contemplating the life of his natal village:

The leather dresser at his perch too stands,
And the keen knife employs his busy hands.
While the neat glover seated at the door
Or in the porch, employs the busy hour.

Or meditating upon the wider West Country prospects that open so spaciously to the view of the wayfarer from the summit of this green hill of legend and romance.

As children, when the floods were out in the Christmas holidays and the half of the county of Somerset would lie before us white as a sheet, there would often be good skating in the meadows of Ilchester, and I remember well when we were returning from one of these expeditions along the main street of the old Parliamentary Borough town noticing how Montacute Hill appeared precisely placed in the centre of the wintry horizon as though, in fact, it had been deliberately set to embellish the landscape outline so sharply segmented by the parallel roofs that bordered the old thoroughfare—the Roman road straight as a pike-staff, and in the exact centre of our vision five miles away the familiar pyramidal hill of our home. The form of a hill of so singular a symmetry must have been well known to the legionaries, and later to the Saxons, especially in those dark days when the fortifications of the Conqueror's 'insatiable brother' began to show themselves upon the hill's crest. Roger Bacon must have known its shape well, as also many a gaoler from the notorious 'Den' in their off hours; to say nothing of generations of humbler folk—waggoners trudging behind wains of loaded hay, drovers at the tails of shambling water-meadow bullocks fat as butter, white bonneted women with balanced buckets of well-water at their arm's ends, and children with marbles and coloured whip-tops in their pockets.

If St Michael's hill has been a diurnal object of vision to the townsmen of Ilchester, how much more to the actual dwellers in Montacute! All the dead who for century after century have been gathered into the church-

Two views of Montacute Hill, with and without the Scotch firs recalled by Llewelyn Powys: 'lofty, haggard trees which offered a sanctuary to every kind of bird, but especially to rooks.' (Photos: Alan Clark and Somerset County Council)

yard of St Catherine's, from the oldest grave to the newest grave, must have known and deeply loved its quiet presence so strong and so unchanging. What the eternal hills of the Promised Land were to the imagination of the dying and exiled Israel, and what the Acropolis was to the Athenians, Miles Hill, this symbol of the enduring earth, has been to the people of Montacute. How many Phelipses, lying now in their family vault near the church porch, must have looked up at its lofty height from the oriels of their proud gallery; how many quarrymen and gloving women must have glanced up at it through twilight window panes. Mrs William Phelips used to tell how a former lady of Montacute House, Dame Betty I think she was called, had herself planted the hill with the forest trees that flourished in so much glory at the end of the nineteenth century. Every afternoon she had carried acorns, chestnuts, or nursery slips to the cherished slopes. What a splendour, if the story is true, the lady's patient task bequeathed to later generations. Well do I remember the hill in its leafy magnificence. The winding trackway that led eventually to the tower was over-shadowed with timber of enormous proportions 'enfolding sunny spots of greenery'. The hill's top was crowned with Scotch firs—lofty, haggard trees that had confronted many an autumn gale and the tallest of which, a veritable forest king, was eventually struck down, a wild cross of

Leodgaresburgh laid at its length, a mass of splintered deal for fools to wonder at.

How impressive an eminence it was in those days, the green mountain which in winter and in summer so utterly dominated the village of golden stones below. The great trees offered sanctuary to every kind of bird, but especially to rooks. Montacute Hill was famed for possessing the largest King-rookery in all Somerset and perhaps in all the west of England. In the winter thousands upon thousands of these birds would come here to roost. On wild autumn nights, at an hour when lamps were being lit, it was scarcely possible to hear oneself speak in the Montacute streets so great would be the clamour set up by the hosts of birds that were passing across the sky.

How we used to watch them from our nursery window—rising and falling, crying and calling, with outstretched ragged wings. It was impossible not to believe that each single one of these fowls was experiencing through bone and feather some strange ecstasy, each quill of them tingling to the whistling squalls, each air-filled bone of them full of the storm's frenzy, full of the frenzy of the great west wind, of the rainy wind, sweeping in from the sea, in from the Bishop rocks, and in from the uncharted wastes of the Atlantic, where masterless oceanic roarers thundered and screamed beneath a scudding sky of grey desolation. Before such tumults the huge trees would sway backwards and forwards delivering themselves of hoarse lamentations, their vexed branches thick clustered all night long with venerable hopper-crows whose beaks were polished white as silver by the constant exercise of corn-stealing from every ground between Avalon and Camelot and Babylon Hill and Pilsden Pen.

On calm evenings, when the smoke was rising straight and blue from the Montacute chimneys, the rooks would fly directly to their roosting place with scarce a caw, but should snow be falling they would be affected as much as they were by rainy winds. In such weather their voices would sound out of the sky with a terrifying resonance as the flakes fell thickly and more thickly—the multitudinous voices of these sapient birds, blacker in colour than Satan, who were performing some strange saraband of their own amidst the white falling goose-feathers from the Polden Hills.

> *Polden Hills are plucking their geese*
> *Faster, faster, faster.*

The magnificent timber had reached to its maturity and the Squire decided eventually to let loose the lumber men into that virginal abode of leaf and branch and bough. In a year's time the hill had been rendered as bald as a skull. Under this abomination of desolation the winter palace of the rook tribe was utterly destroyed. The birds were dispersed and began to form inconsequent colonies wherever they could find a few high trees—in the spinney by the Mill, in the beech trees surrounding John

Scott's old house, and more especially in the half grown spruces that adorned the neighbouring height of Hedgecock. I am told that the tower of St Michael's Mount is once again hidden by timber, but for more than a quarter of a century it remained confronting sun, moon, and stars as lonely as a unicorn's horn. The lesser vegetation was altered also. In the place of the garlic, with its broad green lily-of-the-valley-like leaves which used to carpet the damp forest floor under the attic nurseries of the rooks, there suddenly appeared masses of a new and unfamilar growth, the habit of which rivalled in height the Jerusalem artichokes that prospered each autumn at the bottom of our garden. We children were amazed by the springing up of this unexpected jungle almost tropical in its density. The stalks of the plant were large and stout and in a very special way served our turn for lances to play with. At a loss to know what manner of vegetation they belonged to we persuaded our father to come and inspect this new gigantic wort. He pronounced the plant to be hemlock, but whether it was the same weed out of which the poison given to Socrates was brewed I do not know.

In the immediate neighbourhood of Montacute there are many woods, copses, and spinneys. Indeed the Montacute meadows may be said to be over-shadowed, nay, embowered by a hundred flower-growing retreats. In Summer House Wood periwinkles can be found in February. In Horses Covert on the Eve of St Mark anemones and primroses jostle each other in mossy tree-trunk lawns. In early June the trees of Park Covert shelter wide levels of bluebells as though their trembling leaves were suspended above mirage lakes of ineffable grace. There is no one of these sylvan haunts, however, that has so strong a hold upon the imagination of the Montacute folk as Miles Hill. In a peculiar way this wooded Tor seems to belong to them and they to it. Silently, solemnly it has watched over the village through the long centuries. Club Day after Club Day it has witnessed, with the Kingsbury band playing the Kingsbury jig along the historic streets to the dancing gladness of boy and girl. On cold starlight nights the echoes of the ringers practising have drifted past its dim timber into the farthest borders of space. Each Sunday morning the bells of St Catherine have knolled to church. On the great tenor bell these words are engraved in an ancient lettering: 'He that hearest me to sound, Let him alwaies praise the Lord.' Wedding feast has followed wedding feast, and funeral procession, funeral procession—an unceasing evidence of the fleeting nature of life in the valley below. Proud painted peacocks have screamed at the west wind and cocks have crowed at the sun's rising over Vagg Farm. Men and women have laughed and wept and hated and loved each other year after year, and all has taken place under the shelter of a hill of beauty that is looked upon every day with unmindful familiarity by the tillers and the reapers of the most fertile acreage of Somerset.

'Weymouth . . . before the Esplanade had been disfigured, when the street and the parade were separated by a looped chain suspended from a succession of squat monoliths of Portland stone.' (Photo: Victoria Acland)

Below: 'Club Day after Club Day, with the Kingsbury band playing the Kingsbury jig along the historic streets.' (Photo: Alan Clark)

WEYMOUTH IN THE THREE EIGHTS

WHEN I WAS A CHILD THERE USED TO BE A GREAT EXCITEMENT if a seagull flew over the garden of our home in Somerset. We were accustomed to cock-pheasants, rooks, blackbirds, and fly-catchers, but not to these hungry birds of the winds and waves. Far up above the acacia, above the lawns and sunny flower-beds, they would pass with deliberate purpose on their way back to the sea.

In those days we children knew of only one sea—Weymouth Bay! Clearly I remember how it first suddenly appeared to me as I came up King Street—a wide field of bright-blue water under a curved and cloudless sky. My grandmother lived in a brick house at the further end of Brunswick Terrace, and while my mother, together with "the little ones" and the luggage, was being conveyed there in the old horse-drawn bus of the Burdon Hotel, I had been allowed to walk along the front with my nurse Emily Clare.

A peculiar glamour hangs over my memories of Weymouth in the year 1888. There must have been many inhabitants living then in the royal watering-place who remembered the battle of Waterloo; and truly the look of the "Boscawen," and the look of the huge frigates, their bulging white sails so often visible on the horizon, could not help suggesting to an imaginative mind the Dorset of Captain Hardy and King George III!

To leave the seclusion of Montacute to come to Weymouth was to feel oneself surrounded by the romance of English history. The man who brought buckets of sea water to Penn House every morning had been, so we were always told, a great favourite with our Uncle Littleton, a soldier who had died in India before I was born. This water-carrier had an iron hook in place of the hand which he had lost in battle. What a sight it was on Sundays, standing at the window below the venetian blinds which smelt of sunshine and seaside dust, to watch the after-church procession pass along the Esplanade; the red coats with their swaggering gallantry who were, so I liked to imagine, part of the garrison of the Nothe, of the Nothe that in my eyes was the most perfect model of all forts, with a real portcullis, and real sentries, and real iron cannons of the Napoleonic wars; while everywhere interspersed amongst the soldiers with their pouting red chests, would-be blue-jackets, easy, free, and loose-limbed as cats, idling after the girls. This was before the Esplanade had been disfigured by modern utilitarian shelters, when the street and the parade were separated by a looped chain suspended from a succession of squat monoliths of Portland stone, which in the morning sunshine as I went by them with spade and bucket, would gleam with dazzling seaside whiteness.

Life was less efficient in those days, but surely it passed more pleasantly. It held for me many mysteries, some of which even now continue to perplex my mind. How, for instance, was it possible for the common earth above St John's gardens to conceal real crystals, veritable moonstones fit to be set in silver? When my father first initiated me into this unsuspected secret I was amazed, and to this day when I look out of the East Chaldon carrier's van at the smart villas now built upon this treasure site of my childhood I can hardly trust my memory. It was also the custom of my father to bring back from Portland, that far-distant island, well-selected round flat pebbles far larger than any I had ever seen and on which it was my grandmother's delight to paint pictures of Stalbridge Cross and the Lake of Geneva! Then there were the cowries I used to find, tiny cowries smooth as ivory, with my new playmate, Kitty Steel, the sight of whom at the end of the terrace would set my infant's heart fluttering, so early did I seem to appreciate the sweet symbolism of our spindrift trophies.

In my child's mind the sea front was always separated into two strict divisions. To the right as I came out of the door was all the gaiety of a Vanity Fair, with varnished pleasure boats, entertainment shows, fairy-story goat-carriages, and white flat happy sands good for building castles. To the left was a more sombre expanse where the sea was rough and had to be kept by banks of heavy pebbles from breaking over into Lodmoor, that wild waste of bird-haunted marshland. It was upon the top of these great beaches to the more serious east that real fishing boats were stabled, true deep-sea fishing-boats hollow and benched. Near them I had once seen a draught of fishes brought to land in an encircling net buoyed with corks and strained to breaking-point, a harvest of silver light leaping against the stout black mesh, just as the fish were represented as doing in the Bible picture-book kept in the Sunday cupboard at home.

It was on the other side of the old Red Post, which for many years marked the place where bathing from the beach was allowed, that my father took me one morning to bathe. The importance of wetting my head against the sun's heat had already been impressed upon me and as I walked by my father's side along the sea-path, for in those days the Esplanade did not extend to Greenhill Terrace, I resolved to obey this inexorable mandate by voluntarily lying prostrate at the water's edge until some harmless wave such as I was looking at would wash over me without violence. Alas! When all was ready and I stood prepared to put my plan into action I simply could not do it. The sea seemed so cold, so large, so strong. My father observed my hesitation, and, lifting me into his arms began like a Gulliver, or a benevolent Giant Grumble, to stride forward into the deeper water that separated the shore from "the first sandbank." When the waves were as high as his chest he deliberately lowered his arms until I was entirely submerged. This "ducking" was so terrifying to me that I swallowed an incredible amount of salt water and in consequence was violently sick. It was now my father's turn to feel alarm, and in a very little time I was being carried with tender concern back to my mother. An inhibition about any form of "ducking" has remained with me ever since. At Sherborne I learned to swim, but never to dive, and even now I seldom fail to hold my nose and shut my mouth tight before putting my head under water.

One day I was taken by Emily to ride a donkey. This had been a great ambition with me. All went well in spite of the unexpected jolting. A barefooted nut-brown boy ran at my side. We had gone in the direction of the pier where there were not so many people. I found difficulty in turning the donkey and on one of these occasions my companion who was older than I tugged fiercely at the bridle, in doing which he broke a strap. "You will be put in gaol for this," he said, adding significantly: "You wait till I tell Masser." I immediately appreciated the predicament I was in. With such a consummate liar as sole witness of what had happened I was convinced that the liberty of my person was in grave jeopardy. I was only four years old, but already an infant Ulysses, I had learned to "contrive in my heart," so that as soon as ever we returned to the stand, before the boy had had a chance to speak his winged words, I had slipped off the back of my ass, hurried on to the Esplanade, and in a trice edged myself into the very centre of a crowd that was engaged in watching a Punch-and-Judy show. All that afternoon a distracted search was made for me, but it was not until well on in the evening that I judged it prudent to begin sauntering back to Brunswick Terrace.

My grandmother was a fragile old lady of eighty. She used to lie in a great bed that looked out over the sea, a delicate and brittle doll, her unwrinkled cheeks lightly flushed with a faint pink colour such as is to be seen sometimes on the inside surface of a shell. When I was taken to visit her she would show me pictures. On these occasions I would be placed on her bed. Her frilled pillows always smelt of rosewater and dried lavender. She would show me albums of old-fashioned frosted Christmas cards and faint water-colour sketches of the white cliffs she could see from her window stretching away as far as St Aldhelm's Head.

It is hard for the mind of a child to accommodate itself to the austere ordinance by which all things are determined. My mother used to teach me that if I had sufficient faith my prayers could move mountains, and every morning and evening for many weeks I remember supplicating my father's God to make my grandmother so strong and well that she would be able to carry me pick-a-back across the "ante-room". It was an innocent confidence, but not any more innocent perhaps than the happy beliefs entertained by this old lady who, when the rising moon shone bright upon Weymouth Bay, would often declare that its path was paved with sheets of gold in preparation for her journey to Heaven.

A SOMERSET CHRISTMAS

T WOULD BE A MISTAKE TO IMAGINE THAT OLD PEOPLE CANNOT enjoy the feast of Christmas. Many a grandfather and many a grandmother, seated close and quiet by the fire amid the revelries of children and young people, enter with their long, long memories more deeply into the true spirit of the night than do their light-hearted descendants for all their shining eyes, tossing curls, and merry mistletoe-laughing voices.

Yet Christmas remains, in its essence, the special festival of the young. It is they who possess imaginations sensitive enough to respond with unspoilt eagerness to the glamour of the day. In my own case it has been most certainly so, and with the remembrance of half a century of Christmases held in my mind, it is to the first twenty that I look back with the most joy. My brother Bertie and I would begin to be aware of the approach of Christmas even before the end of the autumn term at Sherborne. We used, I remember, to walk to a certain holly tree growing in the field to the right of Babylon Hill from which we could look across the town of Yeovil to the leafless outlines of Odcombe, Montacute Hill, Hedgecock, and Ham Hill fretted in a miniature landscape on the wintry western horizon. This last-Sunday-of-the-term ritual we performed in a mood of exultant anticipation of the Christmas holidays.

No Christmas Day could have been passed more simply and innocently than ours was at Montacute Vicarage, and yet in retrospect every moment of it seems to have been full of an indescribable golden happiness. The celebrations had their beginning on Christmas Eve with the decorating of the horns in the hall and the pictures in the dining-room. All the day long my brother and I would have been busy collecting, in two large baker's baskets, moss and fir branches for the church, and holly and mistletoe for our own home. The best branches of mistletoe in the glebe orchard we had marked down at the end of the summer holidays when the ground was still thick-strewn with over-ripe, wasp-eaten apples, but these we kept for our requirements at home, and in truth I do not think the pious ladies who were so busy with the pulpit and lectern and windows and pews of St Catherine's, would have welcomed the strange white-berried plant, the very look of whose horned Pagan leaves is remote from ecclesiastical sentiment.

At midnight, with the appearance of the carol singers, the real Christmas celebrations would begin. The men—masons, farm labourers, quarrymen, and gardeners—would stand with their lanterns outside the front door to sing 'Joy to the World', a Christmas carol, the words and music of which had been composed by the delicate genius of Thomas Shoel. At the first notes of the concertina, flute, and harmonium sounding along the dark rambling passage of the silent house, we children would hasten to the dining-room, and collecting on the sofa, wrapped in dressing-gowns and blankets, would peer out into the darkness to see what we might see of the dim dignified figures of old Geard, of Mr William Johnston, of Charley Blake, of Russ, and of a score of other notable personalities familiar enough in the streets of Montacute forty years ago. How strange it was to look out upon the drive, with the tennis lawn obscurely visible beyond the wicker-work fence, and to hear the ancient strains redolent of man's desperate hopes, rise up from the secure Victorian garden into the sky, into eternity! The nativity music would be brought to an end at last with the words 'A merry Christmas and a happy New Year', and afterwards we would hear the opening of the window upstairs, followed by the sound of our father's voice giving the men his thanks and good wishes for the season as he stood in his nightgown by the old broad family bed.

Only a few hours would be allowed to go by in a dreamless sleep and then my brother and I would light candles at our bedside and would begin to examine our stockings—stockings that still contained scraps of lichen from the trunks of the apple trees up which we had swarmed the day before. With our cheeks crammed, like the cheeks of monkeys, with sugar biscuits and sweetmeats, we would occupy ourselves with our presents until the moment came to hurry down to prayers in the dining-room, into which the winter sun, half-way through breakfast, would suddenly penetrate, shining between the naked beech trees that surrounded John Scott's house, from a round ball red as a ruby. John Scott acted as huntsman for one of the Squires for many years. He is buried in the Montacute Churchyard. An epitaph on his stone reads:

> *Here lies John Scott!*
> *It was his lot*
> *A huntsman bold to be*
> *He loved his can*
> *Like any man,*
> *And drank like a fish in the sea.*

At the foot of this ribald drinking doggerel may be read these two curt lines, said to have been carved on the disreputable stone at the order of one of the Bishops of Bath and Wells:

> *And now, God wot,*
> *He has got his lot.*

The old house in Dunster's Orchard has recently, I understand, been demolished. The late Mr Wyndham Goodden could remember when it was inhabited, but it was in ruins when I knew it.

It was typical of those spacious, old-fashioned, genial decades that the first happy meal of the day should each year have been regularly interrupted by a card sent up to the Vicarage by the famous old liberal Baptist minister, the Rev Henry Hardin, with greetings to my father. After breakfast we were free till the morning service, but on such a day, with the familiar chapter from Isaiah, 'Unto us a Child is born', and with the singing of 'While shepherds watched their flocks by night', even being in church was not irksome, especially if my brother Bertie and I, owing to the largeness of our family gathering, were allowed to enjoy the novel experience of sitting on the row of chairs by the Phelips' monuments, where we could whisper to each other and meditate upon Mrs Hodder's turkey that had been hanging 'in the pride of its grease' head downwards in the larder for the last week. After we were home again and the turkey, surrounded by sausages—Maynard's sausages, thin, crisp, bursted, and sizzling, such as I have never tasted since—had been devoured, with the mince-pies and a plum-pudding decorated with a spray of holly, red as a cock's comb, we would gather to have the contents of the Christmas hamper, sent by our Norwich aunts, distributed amongst us by our father, each of us holding out our hands with eager self-interest. Then in the late evening, after our turkey thirst had been thoroughly quenched at the family tea-table, where we all sat snug around the tall oil-lamp, warm behind heavy winter curtains, the hall bell would ring to announce that the Christmas-tree was ready in the school-room.

This was the most valued part of the whole day. It was on the Christmas-tree that we hung the presents that we gave to each other. The tree was dug up every Christmas and replanted the next morning, and seemed little the worse for its annual visit to the house. And how resplendent the spruce sapling would look, upright in its box in the centre of the school-room, in the centre of what in Mr Goodden's day was called 'the servants' hall'. It is odd to remember that the Christmas-tree was practically unknown in England until, by the marriage of Queen Victoria to the Prince Consort, the custom was introduced from Germany, its kinship perhaps with unrecorded fire-worshipping practices rendering this primitive ritual easily acceptable, even in so conservative an island as England, used for time out of mind to the burning of a yule log.

In an hour the floor would be littered with tinsel paper and the coloured candles would be flaring low in their sockets, till, one after another, a feathered fir twig would fill the room with the incense of the wild forest. Then the moment would come when, with crossed arms, we would dance in a ring about the innocent tree, singing 'Auld Lang Syne.' I can even now, in my mind's eye, see the tall figure of my father, with child-like benedictions emanating from his good face, as our voices rose and fell loud enough to be heard out on the cold deserted allotment plots where parcels of roughed-up wintry ground were waiting to be re-dug for the planting on Good Friday of well-sprouted potato seedlings. As we swayed backwards and forwards about the tree with laughing voices, not one of us, I suppose, was cognizant of the calm processes of nature which were taking place around the house—the grasses on the lawn sparkling as brightly as the stars in the heaven, while beneath the comfortable slate roof of Montacute Vicarage the lives of old and young were passing away under the shadow of God's irreversible ordinance.

Other Books of West Country interest

Redcliffe Press are the leading publishers of books on Somerset and Avon, with more in course of preparation.

The following is a selection of our West Country titles:

Somerset Scrapbook by Joan Astell £2.95

Evokes life in the county before the mass ownership of the motor car: a world of quiet roads, lonely farms and isolated villages. Photographs from the remarkable Alfred Vowles collection.

Somerset at Work: 1870-1950 by Joan Astell £3.50

Superb selection of archive photographs, many previously unpublished. Gives a fascinating picture of the skills and crafts of Somerset people in a surprising range of occupations.

Somerset & Avon Ghosts, Witches and Legends by John Bailey £1.95

Journalist John Bailey graphically retells the stories of 27 mysterious happenings. From the macabre resurrection of a 16th century corpse to ghostly sightings by motorists on the A370 at Congresbury, all are treated with an entertaining mixture of journalistic scepticism and wry humour.

Old Somerset Customs by Muriel Walker £1.95

Somerset is rich in ancient customs, folklore and superstitions. Collop Monday, the Tatworth candle auction, the Minehead hobby-horse, orchard wassailing . . . these and many more Somerset customs are brought vividly to life in a collection which will delight residents and visitor alike.

Weston-Super-Mare: Good Old Days by John Bailey £1.95

Who better to tell the story of the famous seaside resort than the man who edited the *Weston Mercury* for twenty years? Packed with fascinating and amusing anecdotes and over 50 nostalgic photographs.

Sacred & Satiric by J.H. Bettey and C.W.G. Taylor £2.25

The story of the stone carvings in West Country churches—their subjects ranging from the deeply religious to the monstrous and grotesque.

Profusely illustrated from churches in Somerset, Avon, Gloucestershire and Wiltshire.

Bath by Edith Sitwell hardback £8.95

At last—a new edition of the celebrated study of eighteenth century social life in Bath. Captures the atmosphere of the times superbly, with Beau Nash and all the famous personalities who graced the period with their wit, their beauty and their eccentricity.

The illustrations include Rowlandson's 'Comforts of Bath'.

Bath: Profile of a City by Paul Hardy and William Lowndes
£4.95

Superb drawings of many of Bath's finest buildings, and some lesser known gems, with brilliant 'pen portraits' giving the stories of the people who lived there.

Dorset Essays by Llewelyn Powys hardback £6.95

An evocation of the Dorset countryside and its people in the early years of this century, by a modern master of English prose writing. Photographs by Ann Clarke.

Thirteen Worthies By Llewelyn Powys £2.50

From Chaucer to Hardy, a collection of delightful vignettes of men whose lives the author found admirable and interesting—including the Dorset poet William Barnes, and Tom Coryat, born in the Somerset village of Odcombe in 1577 and later to be the eccentric chronicler of travels on foot in Europe and Asia.

Skin for Skin by Llewelyn Powys £1.75

First published in 1926, this West Country classic recalls life in the Edwardian era. Chapters on Montacute, the Dorset and Somerset countryside, a stay with brother T.F. Powys in the village of East Chaldon and recollections of Christmas and New Year's Eve.

Earth Memories by Llewelyn Powys hardback £6.95

This collection contains many of Powys' finest country essays, including 'The Other Side of the Quantocks' and the author's first visit, in search of family memories, to the Dorset village of Stalbridge. With introduction by Philip Larkin.

West Country Stone Walls by Janet Bodman £1.35

A unique county-by-county survey of the stones, patterns and techniques used for centuries by craftsmen building in natural stone, from Bristol to Land's End.

The 12 colour photographs (and 14 in black and white) complement the author's descriptions of the many beautiful colours to be found in some of the walls.

Wookey: The Caves Beyond by Martin Farr £1.50

The gripping story of cave diving at Wookey Hole. The author is a noted diver himself, as well as being an internationally famed underwater photographer.

Please ask your bookseller about any of these books. In case of difficulty, they may be obtained direct from Redcliffe Press Ltd., 49 Park Street, Bristol BS1 5NT, enclosing your cheque. Please add carriage of 75p for order up to £5, and £1 on orders over £5.
A catalogue of our full list of West Country titles is also available.